TYRONE
FOLK
TALES

T0346854

TYRONE
FOLK
TALES

DOREEN McBRIDE

The
History
Press

First published 2016

The History Press
97 St George's Place, Cheltenham,
Gloucestershire GL50 3QB
www.thehistorypress.co.uk

British Library Cataloguing in Publication Data.
A catalogue record for this book is available from the British Library.

ISBN 978 1 84588 230 3

Typesetting and origination by The History Press
Printed by TJ Books Limited, Padstow, Cornwall

CONTENTS

PREFACE

In May 2015 I led a bus tour of historic sites for the Queen's University Women's Common Room Club. Vicious showers had greeted us at our first stop, Castlecaulfield, but the sky began to clear as we stepped out into a modest car park off the Tullywiggan Road between Cookstown and Stewartstown. As we climbed up Tullyhogue Hill, we all seemed to realise that this is a special place, steeped in history. At the top is an Iron Age rath, an enclosed earthen fort surrounded by two great banks and two deep ditches. This was neither a dwelling place nor a place to be defended – except, very likely, from the assault of spirits from the other world. Once the capital of the Uí Tuirtre of Airgialla, this was for centuries the inauguration site of the O'Neills, the lords of Tír Eoghain. Here the Lord O'Cahan threw a golden shoe over the head of the O'Neill seated on Leac na Rí and then the Lord O'Hagan, custodian of Tullyhogue, picked up the shoe, placed it on one of O'Neill's feet and handed him the rod of office. This was memorably sketched by Richard Bartlett, who also recorded the smashing of the inauguration stone by Lord Mountjoy as Hugh O'Neill's rebellion was in its final stages in 1602.

After admiring the great trees and the last of the bluebells on the summit, my tour group looked out over an awe-inspiring panorama of a great sweep of Ulster. If they hadn't realised it already, they learned then that Tyrone is a very beautiful county. They were particularly struck by the sight of the waters of Lough Neagh due east, the Antrim plateau beyond it, the volcanic plug of Slemish and, to the north, the rounded slopes of the Sperrins. Their eyes were on land that had been soaked in history and legend from the very earliest times.

Doreen McBride's book draws on rich veins, the lore of peoples who have lived out their lives in County Tyrone for millennia. Could some of the stories of the supernatural she relates go back to the Bronze Age inhabitants who left extraordinary stone circles, cairns and alignments at Beaghmore? Or those who constructed and carved the Knockmany Passage Grave? Or those who crafted Ardboe Cross? Or Harry Avery's mighty castle, erected by Henrí Aimhréidh Ó Néill in the fourteenth century? Or the Plantation castles at Benburb, Castlederg and Castlecaulfield? Or those who worshipped in secret at the Reaskmore Mass Rock? Or the privileged residents of Lissan House?

The tales recorded by Doreen – no matter how fanciful or outlandish – have been passed down by word of mouth, in some cases for generations. I am pleased to see the inclusion of four stories by William Carleton, born in Prillisk in 1794. He painted a vivid picture of life in pre-Famine Ulster. He delights in availing of local dialect and uses some of the words catalogued by Doreen. Many are new to me, including 'elf-shot' and 'dilsy'. I am also glad that the genius of Flann O'Brien/Myles na gCopaleen is duly recognised. I recommend 'Lough Neagh: The Source of Mystery and Legend' and I mourn the extinction of the great lake's arctic char (I blame run-off from eighteenth-century lint holes and nineteenth-century bleach works).

A great merit of Doreen McBride's book is that it does not have to be methodically read from start to finish. The volume can be opened anywhere, by the fireside, in bed, wherever … and why not read out snippets for the entertainment of family and friends? This is an entertaining and informative book. Enjoy.

Jonathan Bardon, 2016

ACKNOWLEDGEMENTS

Thanks are due to my husband, George, who insisted on coming with me to do research, to 'protect' me because I ask 'innocent strangers so many fool questions' that somebody some day is bound to think I'm 'away in the head' and lock me up. He also uncovered a lot of interesting information.

On a more serious note, thanks are due to my cousin, Vernon Finlay, for reading the text and making very helpful comments.

Thanks are also due to Sally Skilling, assistant librarian at the Ulster Folk and Transport Museum; the staff of the Irish and Local Studies Library in Armagh; the staff at Strabane Library; the staff at Omagh Library, especially Deidre Nugent; Christine Johnston, librarian at the Mellon Centre of Migration Studies, the Ulster American Folk Park; the Linen Hall Library; Banbridge Library; Dr Jonathan Bell, former Curator of Agriculture at the Ulster Folk and Transport Museum, for information about spades; and Dr Gordon McCoy and Richard Ryan for information about language.

I am grateful to Dr Eamon Phoenix, who is a fount of good stories, good *craic* and fascinating information; Dr Jonathan Bardon for information about sweat houses; Mark Cranwell, a ranger whose work includes Bellaghy Bawn, who told me about Susan, the ghost who haunts the bawn and introduced me to Peter and Mary Craig, who live in the bawn's oldest house and shared their experiences; Evelyn Cardwell for information about mountainy folk; Graham Mawhinney for information about the life and work of Geordie Barnett; Dr Mary Wack, who gave me the story 'Joseph McPherson and the Fairies'; Mark Greenstreet, Sheryl Dillon, George Beattie and Margaret Jones for information; Celia Ferguson for information about Sion Mills and folk cures and the late William Reid's daughters Pamela and Margaret for permission to reproduce 'Calypso Collapse'; the late Crawford Howard for permission 'to do what I wanted' with his work and to his executors for confirming that permission; and to Art O'Dailaigh for sharing the story about the sighting of a ghostly horse near Banbury.

Thanks must go, too, to the staff, especially Paula Ward and John Donaghy, of An Creagán Visitor Centre for arranging a night when local people shared their folklore around a beautiful fire, to Francis Clarke for letting me hear a tape of stories recorded more than twenty-five years ago, to Patrick J. Haughey, who told me some great yarns, and to Cormac McAleer, who aided and abetted the others and added some of his own stories.

I am also grateful to Nick Kennedy for information about Brian O'Nolan, alias Flann O'Brien, to Johnny Dooher and his wife Gabrielle for information about ghosts in Strabane and to Angela O'Connor from Ranfurly Arts Centre for information about the O'Neills. I wish to acknowledge, too, the custodians of the Ulysses Simpson Grant Ancestral Homestead and the late Hannah Simpson, who gave me information about the president and the Mellon banking family. I met her in the 1970s when she lived in the ancestral cottage. Dr Neil Watt provided information about Lissan House, Charlene Mullan and Pat Grimes provided information about Ardboe and Lough Neagh. Richard Knox gave me information about W.F. Marshall and the Marshall family kindly gave me permission to print 'Me and Me Da'.

Finally, my thanks go to Rachel Barlow for drawing the illustration on page 114.

INTRODUCTION

The name 'Tyrone' came from *Tír Eoghain*, meaning Eoghain's land. During Celtic times it was referred to as 'Tyrone among the bushes'. Its people are reputed to have 'open hearts and a desire to please' and their folk tales are as varied as their landscape and speech. I found it a fascinating, haunted place with roots stretching back into antiquity.

The late W.F. Marshall, who was elected a Member of the Royal Irish Academy in 1942 in recognition of his work on language, said local Ulster dialects preserve much of the grammar, style, vocabulary and word order of the sixteenth and seventeenth centuries and so the dialects spoken in County Tyrone are not a corruption of English; they are the roots of something much older, which forms a museum of language.

The sixteenth and seventeenth centuries were troubled times in Ireland because the Catholic Philippe of Spain believed he was the rightful owner of the English throne. He believed the English throne should have passed to him on the death of his wife, Queen Mary I, not to her sister, Elizabeth I. Queen Elizabeth disagreed, realised Ireland was a back door through which her country could be attacked and waged a war in Ireland the likes of which had never been seen. She won, but that didn't do her much good because she was dead when the news reached her! The news of her death didn't reach her generals until after they'd enforced a harsh peace settlement on the Earls of Ulster, causing them to flee, an act which became known as 'The Flight of the Earls'. This left Ulster, the last Irish province to be captured by the English, without leaders and open to the Plantation of Ulster. Tyrone and Fermanagh were the only two counties to be planted and their history is reflected in their folk tales.

I was amazed by the differences I found between Fermanagh folk tales and Tyrone folk tales. They are adjacent counties and both were planted, so I expected their stories to be similar. I could not have been more wrong. I found the occasional ghost story in Fermanagh, but Tyrone is full of ghosts! I suspect it's the most haunted county in Ireland, but fortunately most of the ghosts are benign and don't do any harm. Another thing that surprised me was the close link Tyrone appears to have with Donegal, which although it is part of the province of Ulster, is situated in another country, namely the Republic of Ireland, not the United Kingdom.

Tyrone is the largest county in Ulster. I feel I entered four different worlds during the time I was doing research. Each one was as enchanting as the last and I'm very grateful to the many 'innocent bystanders', as my husband called them, for the pleasant, friendly way in which they helped me.

TYRONE AMONG THE BUSHES

The following poem, 'Tyrone Among the Bushes' by Edith Wheeler, was published in The Sacred Heart Review, *Volume 30, No. 21, 21 November 1903.*

I'm weary of the city ways, the hurry, din and bustle,
I'm weary of the scorchin' heat, the crowds that gape and hustle;
I'm longing for a bit of green, the quiet evening hushes
In my own land, my homeland, Tyrone among the Bushes.

I hate the groomed-up city swells, the way they have of talkin';
I hate the look of city belles, their flouncy style of walkin';
I'd like to hear the colleens speak with tongues as sweet as threshes,
With modest eyes and quiet mien in Tyrone among the Bushes.

I'd give my soul to sit again beside the fire at even',
And see the neighbors gather round, their fancy tales of weavin';
Ye'd wonder for to see them here, with balls and spreads and crushes,
We'll learn them what's Society in Tyrone among the Bushes.

Edith Wheeler

1

THE GHOSTS OF LISSAN HOUSE

County Tyrone is undoubtedly beautiful, with a varied landscape and a strange haunting atmosphere. One can almost feel the presence of the souls of the dead who have lived, and loved, there in the past. Many respectable people have, over the ages, reported seeing ghosts in circumstances that cannot simply be dismissed.

Thanks are due to Dr Neil Watt, for the following tales about the ghosts who haunt Lissan House.

Lissan House dates back to the early seventeenth century. It was owned by the Staples family, who were planters. It is in the heart of an ancient area called Glenkonkyne, a densely wooded district thought to have been used for religious ceremonial purposes in the past. It was once ruled by the O'Neills, who were the Kings of Ulster and as a result it embraces the cultures of both planter and Gael.

One of the owners of the house, Sir Robert Ponsonby Staples, was a well-known painter. Many of his drawings and sketches may still be seen in the property.

Sir Robert was an eccentric who believed many of the ills of his generation were caused by wearing shoes. He thought they interfered with 'healing magnetism' coming up from the earth and insisted people walk about the house in their bare feet.

In the mid-nineteenth century, Sir Thomas Staples inherited Lissan House. He had a very beautiful wife, Lady Katherine Staples, known as handsome Kitty Staples. She loved music, spending money and entertaining but unfortunately she was unable to have children. Her husband died years before she did and the heir to the property was a nephew of her husband, Nathaniel Staples, who lived in India. When dilsy Lady Katherine and Nathaniel Staples met, it was hate at first sight! They simply could not stand each other so when she moved out of the house she took all the furniture, light fittings and doors with her. Her nephew was left with nothing but a worthless, empty shell. She's not a happy ghost because her action annoyed the other spirits haunting the house. They loved their old home and were furious with her. It is said her action led to a reversal in the fortunes of the Staples family. They lost a lot of money and no longer have the high place in society they once held.

A well-known artist painted a portrait of handsome Kitty Staples in her prime. When she died it was given to her god-daughter and eventually ended up in an auction. The Lissan House Trust bought it and hung it up on the drawing room wall. The minute it was put in place Nathaniel's portrait fell off the wall. There was no reason for this as it was hung on secure wires and the hooks on the wall were intact. The dislike they had for each other on earth must be continuing through eternity!

Hazel Radclyffe Dolling, the last member of the Staples family to live in the house, died, aged 82, in 2006 and had many strange tales to tell about the ghostly goings-on in her home. Certain parts of the house suddenly become cold, the heavy footsteps of an invisible man or a small child's sobs might be heard and sometimes it is possible to smell lavender and rose petals. One house guest saw a group of noisy children playing in the hall. She wondered who they were and walked towards them to ask, but they skipped off down the hall and then vanished into thin air.

Dr Neil Watt, the present manager of Lissan House, insists he did not believe in ghosts until he went to work in the house in 2013. He has since changed his mind because of his experiences! The first was when he was working during the first Christmas after which he'd been appointed as curator. He'd gone into the garden and collected holly and ivy to be used as decorations. He'd been working for a long time and became very hungry so he phoned his sister and asked if she'd bring him a Chinese takeaway. She is a medical doctor, a very sensible, down-to-earth, practical person. She agreed, bought a takeaway, drove up the drive and parked her car in front of a drawing room window. She entered the house, looked at Neil and said, 'Why didn't you tell me you had company? I'd have bought two takeaways.'

When Neil said he was alone she replied, 'You're joking! I saw a podgy young man, dressed in tweeds, standing beside the piano, chatting away to you.' There was nobody there!

Once when Neil was working in the ballroom he heard a dog barking at his feet, a distinct 'Woof! Woof!', the type of bark a dog gives when it wants to be taken for a walk. He was intrigued and did something he thought he'd never do. He asked a medium to come in. She looked at Neil and said, 'You're fond of dogs, aren't you?'

'How did you know?' he asked.

'Because two dogs, a red setter and a terrier, are running around your feet!' she replied.

One of the ghosts in Lissan House caused a bad atmosphere around Lady Staples's bedroom. Both Neil and the chairman of Lissan House felt an unreasonable urge to get out whenever they went into that room! One night the burglar alarm sounded. The chairman came to turn it off and check the premises. As he approached Lady Staples's bedroom, he was suddenly tossed to the ground and hit the skirting board, so Neil and he decided to ask a medium to visit to find out what was happening. She said Alexander Staples, the founder member of the family, loved his old home and was protecting it. He was taking especially good care of Lady Staples's bedroom and was standing, shouting obscene language them. She said, 'The best way to deal with a ghost is to face it. Whenever you feel Alexander's presence talk to him. Tell him you are only looking after the house, you love it too and it needs attention. You're not going to do anything harmful.' Now when Neil goes into Lady Staples's bedroom to carry out basic maintenance he talks to the ghost and feels a right eejit while doing so! But it works!

The last owner of the house, Mrs Dolling, used Lady Staples's bedroom as a guest room. Women who slept in there often reported hearing footsteps. Sometimes a lady, dressed in a gold dress, wearing boots and carrying a doll and a candle, came into the room and tried to set Lady Staples's bed on fire! Perhaps that's why the ghost of Alexander Staples protects it?

Photographers and people walking in the garden often see a little girl, aged between 11 and 12 years old, looking out one of the windows on the top floor. Photographs have been taken of what must be a ghost because there's nobody there! That little girl is very shy. She has never appeared for a medium, although she has often been spotted peeping round corners or hanging over the bannister.

One night when Neil and one of the trustees were setting up a piano in the ballroom they heard two ladies laughing. Neil went on an errand to the far end of the house and, while he was away, the trustee heard chit-chat behind him, yet there was nobody there.

'Be off, or I'll kick you down the stairs!'

2

THE GHOST
OF LORD TYRONE

When I first went to teach in Dromore High School, County Down, some of my pupils asked me if I believed in ghosts. I said, 'Yes. I once lived in a haunted house in Belfast. I never saw the ghost but my mother did. It wasn't an unfriendly presence, just the harmless spirit of a woman who wandered around the house. It was a happy home with a beautiful garden and my family loved it. My parents sold it when it became too big for them after my sister and I married.'

My pupils asked me if I'd like to hear a horrific tale about how the ghost Lord Tyrone appeared to his old friend, Lady Beverage, who was visiting Gilhall, a local stately home said to be the most haunted house in Ireland. It burnt down in 1966.

This is an unusual story because the ghost not only predicted the future accurately, including the age at which Lady Beresford would die, but it left a mark on her wrist, which she kept hidden under a black ribbon. That mark was clearly visible after her death and the story is preserved in the Blacker family papers.

During the latter part of the seventeenth century, Nicola Sophia Hamilton and her cousin John Le Poer were orphaned. They were very young and put into the care of a guardian, who believed in deism, a religious school of thought that holds that the earth was made by God and then left to its own devices to administer itself by natural laws. Deism acknowledges the importance of moral behaviour but rejects any belief in the supernatural and says there is no life after death.

Nicola and John became close friends. At 14 years of age, they suffered another upset when their guardian died. The early teen years are a time when young people are both sensitive and vulnerable. Nicola and John had already supported each other through the pain caused by the death of their parents and now they had another tragedy to contend with. It drew them even closer together.

They were very confused because their new guardian, a sincere Christian, attempted to change what he considered their pagan beliefs. They didn't become Christians but their belief in deism was shaken. Nicola and John, like all teenagers, took life very seriously. They worried about the differences in the religious beliefs taught by each of two well-loved guardians and eventually made a pact. They promised each other that whoever should die first would, if at all possible, come back to earth and tell the other one which was the true religion and if there was life after death.

Nicola married Sir Tristram Beresford of Coleraine in February 1688 and became Lady Beresford while John Le Poer became Lord Tyrone when his father died. He also got married and the two families enjoyed a warm friendship, often spending several weeks in each other's company.

A short time after Lord Tyrone and his family had visited Lady Beresford, she went with her husband to visit her sister, Arabella, who was married to Sir John Magill and lived in Gilhall, near Dromore in County Down. After spending a night there, Lady Beresford came down to breakfast looking pale and exhausted. She was wearing a black band around her wrist. Lord Beresford was a loving husband and felt concerned by his wife's appearance.

'Darling, what's wrong?' he asked. 'You look ill and why are you wearing that black ribbon round your wrist?'

'I'm fine,' she replied. 'I didn't sleep very well. And please promise you won't ask any more questions about my black ribbon. I don't want to talk about it.'

Lord Beresford was puzzled by her behaviour. She kept wondering if the post had arrived yet. Eventually he asked, 'Why are you so concerned about today's post? Are you expecting a letter?' He was shaken to the core by her reply. 'Yes! One that'll tell me John died unexpectedly last Tuesday afternoon.'

'When I asked you do come back and tell me if there's life after death I didn't mean it!'

Later that day the couple were horrified to receive a letter, tied up in a black ribbon, saying that Lord Tyrone had died the previous Tuesday afternoon. Lady Beresford was devastated and clung to her husband saying, 'Dearest, John's ghost came and visited me last night. I thought I was dreaming. He told me we're going to have a son who'll grow up and marry the daughter of Lord Tyrone.' However, she didn't tell him the whole story of how she had awoken during the night to find the ghost of Lord Tyrone sitting on her bed or about the prediction of her husband's and her own deaths or how she'd thought the ghost actually was Lord Tyrone.

'What are you doing here at this hour of the night?' she'd asked.

'I am dead,' he had replied. 'I died last Tuesday. Do you remember that solemn promise we made to each other when we were very young? I've been allowed to keep it and can tell you deism is not the true religion. There is definitely life after death.'

'Stop joking! You're not dead. You look very much alive to me!'

'I'm telling you I'm dead. You'll get a letter tomorrow to tell you.'

'I don't believe you!'

'Well, I'll show you!' he said, and with that the apparition started to move objects around the room. Then he pulled one of the curtains round her four-poster bed up through a loop. (It took several men a considerable amount of time to put it back into its rightful position the next day. It was a difficult job.)

Lady Beresford still didn't believe what she was hearing, so Lord Tyrone's ghost said, 'I repeat, you'll get a letter telling you of my death tomorrow. Shortly after that you'll have a son. Four years later your husband will die and some time after that you'll marry again. Your second marriage will be a big mistake. You'll be very unhappy. You'll have another son and die on your forty-seventh birthday.'

'You can't know all that! I don't believe you. You always were a bit of a joker!'

'I'll make you believe me,' snarled the ghost. He stood up and touched her wrist. He didn't hurt her but the next day the skin appeared burnt and the muscles and ligaments shrivelled, leaving a nasty scar.

'All right! All right!' she gasped. 'I believe you. You're dead. Now tell me, how can I keep from dying when I'm 47?'

'Don't marry again. You'll die shortly after giving birth to another son if you do.'

Lord Tyrone's ghost touched the top of a chest of drawers, then disappeared. The next day, Lady Beresford was horrified to find his fingerprints had burnt into the polished wood.

Lord Beresford died, as predicted, four years later, on 16 June 1701, leaving his wife as a single parent with one son and one daughter. Lady Beresford withdrew from society and led a very quiet life for several years. She didn't see anyone except a clergyman and his wife, who were close friends. The clergyman had a son, Lieutenant Colonel, later

Lieutenant General, Gorges of Kilbrew, who fell in love with her. He was attentive and charming. At first she resisted his advances but he was very persuasive and eventually she agreed to marry him in April 1704. It was, as the ghost of Lord Tyrone had predicted, a big mistake. Her new husband treated her very badly and she was very unhappy. The couple separated for some time then he promised to mend his ways and they were reunited. She became pregnant and gave birth to a son.

The clergyman who had christened her and was a close family friend came to see her after the baby's birth. He found her in great form. She was delighted with her little son and said, 'It's my birthday! I'm 48 years of age today! That means I don't have to worry about dying on my forty-seventh birthday because now I'm 48! That's a relief! I'm older than the age at which Lord Tyrone's ghost said I'd die.'

'I'm afraid you're wrong!' said the clergyman. 'Your mother and I had an argument about your age. She thought you were 48 but I know you're only 47. I went and checked. You were born in 1666. That means I'm right! Today's your forty-seventh birthday!'

Lady Beresford went very white. 'Are you sure?' she quavered.

'Yes! Quite sure.'

'In that case, please leave me. You've signed my death warrant and I have things I must do.' She immediately sent for her son, Marcus, and her close friend, Lady Betty Cobb. She told them how Lord Tyrone had visited her after his death and what he'd done to convince her he really was a ghost. They didn't really believe her extraordinary story and left her alone to rest as she suddenly appeared very tired. When they came back after a few hours they found she was dead. When they unwrapped the black ribbon tied around her wrist they found it was as she described. The skin appeared burnt while the muscles and sinews were shrivelled and wasted.

Marcus did marry Lord Tyrone's daughter as the ghost had foretold. Lady Betty told the Blacker family what had happened and the story was preserved in their papers. During the following years, all sorts of manifestations appeared in the house, which developed the reputation of being the most haunted place in Ireland.

3

HALF-HUNG
MCNAUGHTON

Thanks are due to Celia Ferguson (née Herdman) for telling me about how one of her ancestors was robbed by a highwayman and to Gabrielle Dooher for giving me information about Half-Hung McNaughton.

Half-Hung McNaughton belonged to a wealthy family. He had a good job working for the government as a tax collector but he also had an addiction to gambling. He lost all his own money and started gambling with the government's money. He lost £800 of his employer's cash (the equivalent of about £500,000 today) before disappearing from respectable society to become a highwayman and escape justice.

McNaughton had a very good friend, Andrew Knox, who owned Prehen House in Derry/Londonderry and had a beautiful, 15-year-old daughter called Mary Ann. She became besotted with McNaughton and wanted to marry him. Andrew Knox was very annoyed and forbade the match. He felt that there was too big an age gap between the couple (Mary Ann was only 15 while McNaughton was 39) and that McNaughton's main motivation was to get his hands on her money so he could clear his debts and continue gambling. He decided the best thing he could do was take Mary Ann away and hope she'd forget about her lover. Unfortunately, the girl managed to contact McNaughton by leaving and receiving notes at a tree and he arranged to kidnap her.

McNaughton dressed in his highwayman gear and met the coach in which Mary Ann and her father were travelling. There was a fracas during which McNaughton accidentally shot and killed her. Both he and her father were wounded. He managed to escape but was eventually captured and incarcerated in Lifford jail before being tried. He was sentenced to death 'by hanging on the great road between Strabane and Lifford'. He mounted the gallows and the hangman placed the rope around his neck and attempted to drop him to his death. The rope broke and McNaughton fell to the ground, unhurt. Anyone who survived hanging automatically received a pardon. He could have walked away a free man, but he did no such thing. He picked himself up, climbed back up onto the gallows and shouted, 'I don't want to be pardoned. I don't want to be known as "Half-Hung McNaughton". I don't want to live without Mary Ann. I demand to be hung!' He insisted the hangman's rope be placed around his neck again and jumped off the gallows with such vigour that his neck was broken and he died instantly. His body was buried in St Patrick's old graveyard in Strabane. His ghost is said to haunts the graveyard and the road between Strabane and Derry/Londonderry.

Half-hung McNaughton was an unusual highwayman because nobody appeared to have any respect for him. In the past, taxes and rents were high, much higher than in England. Farmers existed on a knife edge. If they couldn't pay their rent, they were evicted. Most highwaymen robbed from the rich and gave to the poor in the tradition of Robin Hood. They were regarded as folk heroes, protected by the local population. But McNaughton did not share his ill-gotten gains; he kept them. After his death the population split into two camps: those who felt sorry for him and believed he really did love Mary Ann Knox and committed suicide because he couldn't bear to live without her and those who felt he committed suicide to avoid ending up in a debtors' prison, which could have been regarded as a fate worse than death.

Celia Ferguson (*née* Herdman) told me about how one of her ancestors, a doctor called John Herdman, was robbed by a highwayman. One night when he was coming home after visiting a patient, he was attacked and stripped of everything except his shirt! Poor John Herdman was very embarrassed by his state of undress and went to the home of a local parson for help. The parson thought he was a 'rogue and a vagabond' and refused to let him in. John managed to prove he was an educated gentleman man by speaking in Latin. When the highwayman was caught and sentenced to death several years later he confessed on the gallows and apologised for treating John Herdman so badly.

4

WHITE LADIES, BANSHEES AND GHOSTLY PIPERS

Some years ago I went on an outing arranged by the Ulster Federation of Local Studies to Derry/Londonderry. As we travelled along the Londonderry Road towards Strabane I asked our guide (unfortunately I can't remember his name) if he knew of any ghosts haunting the area. He laughed and told me about the ghost who was in Altnagelvin Hospital with fourteen stitches in his head!

The Altnagelvin ghost was inspired by 'a woman', dressed in white, who appeared when a new roundabout was being constructed on the motorway near Toomebridge. She ran along beside the traffic during the twilight hour and waved at the occupants of cars. She caused a sensation! Traffic increased at dusk. The situation became dangerous, with cars full of people driving round and round, hoping to see the ghost. It was obvious there was going to be a serious accident. The ghost's appearance was good for business because people who hoped to see her invariably ended up in a local pub!

Eventually the matter was reported to the police and the ghost was caught. 'She' was a young fellow, with an unfortunate sense of humour, who, at dusk, donned a long blonde wig, used talcum powder to make his hands and face appear white and dressed in a long, flowing, white, Victorian-style nightdress. He was arrested, taken to court, tried and found guilty of disturbing the peace. Fortunately for him, the magistrate had a sense of humour. 'The ghost' received nothing more than a severe dressing down and was bound over to keep the peace.

The guide's brother-in-law reckoned the 'roundabout ghost' had been good for local business in the area, attracting many visitors. As unemployment in Strabane was very high he felt it was time the road between Strabane and Derry/Londonderry had its own ghost. He made himself a large, towering mask, like the ones worn by mummers, covered it with a sheet and went out to do his best for local humanity by haunting the road. Unfortunately he chose a Saturday after which Strabane Gaelic football team had not only played Derry/Londonderry, but had won. There is great rivalry between the two teams. The win was well and truly celebrated, so everyone on the bus was what is locally described as 'half-tore'! They were full of bravado when the ghost appeared and in no mood to be frightened by it. They stopped the bus, got off, ran after it and threw stones. As a result, the poor ghost was badly injured and ended up in Altnagelvin Hospital with fourteen stitches in his head!

The following ghost stories are not so easily explained away.

Packie the Ghost Haunts the Silverbirch Hotel, Omagh

Thanks are due to the receptionist at the Silver Birch Hotel, Omagh, who told me about the hotel's resident ghost, Packie.

Packie was a previous owner of the hotel. He, like the majority of ghosts found in County Tyrone, is not malevolent. He simply walks up and down the corridors of the oldest parts of the hotel and his presence is often felt in the staff office behind the reception desk. Many people have seen his shadow and some have heard him knocking on walls. He tends to appear if the hotel is being renovated or extended. The staff think he's still taking an interest in the business he once owned. There are three different schools of thought among the staff about their resident ghost: those who say the very idea of the existence of spirits from another world is all 'stuff and nonsense'; those who are terrified of ghosts and shiver at the very mention of the supernatural; and others who just laugh and say Packie is welcome – he's not doing anyone any harm.

GHOSTS OF BELLAGHY BAWN

Thanks are due to Mark Cranwell, Peter and Mary Craig and Richard Mulholland for the following ghost stories about Bellaghy Bawn.

Bellaghy Bawn began life as a fortified settlement during the Plantation of Ulster. It was planted with people who were associated with the Vintners Society of London and intended to develop commerce in the area.

Bellaghy itself was an ancient settlement with a long history and great pride in its past. After the Elizabethan Wars, the original inhabitants resented all attempts to change their lifestyle. The planters were forced to live in a well-defended barracks called a 'bawn', which was a group of dwellings built near a good water supply and surrounded by a stout defensive wall. The occupants were wary of venturing out alone, preferring to stay in groups and carry arms for self-defence. Each bawn contained a tower from which enemy movements could be observed and was defended by troops.

Sarah was a very beautiful young local girl who did something that was strictly forbidden. She fell in love with one of the soldiers stationed in the bawn, an action which led to her death. None of my informants knew how she died, but her ghost has been seen moving within the bawn and on occasion she causes the air around a set of outside steps to become freezing cold.

At one time the bawn belonged to people called the Thompsons, who had a cook called Susan. Susan's ghost is said to haunt the old ballroom. She has been seen many times and now usually appears in the room in which videos are shown.

Peter and Mary Craig live in the oldest house on the site, which was built around 1600. They have often been aware of ghostly presences, have heard strange knocking sounds and seen shadows flitting past. At first they thought it was only their imaginations working on the natural creaks and groans of an old building. When their son heard distinct knocking on glass that could not be explained away as a result of the ageing process of an old building, they called in the ghostbusters, who felt a ghostly presence in their bathroom.

Judith Montgomery once stayed in the house and found it very disturbing because her possessions were thrown around her room. She took Peter up to her room once and he saw her things were spread all over the place. She explained that it kept happening and it was very annoying!

Peter said originally that he did not believe in ghosts but so many strange things have happened in the house that he's not so sure now.

A priest was asked to come and sprinkle holy water around the house. That appears to have helped, but neither Sarah nor Peter feel confident that the ghosts have gone for good!

At present Bellaghy Bawn contains a museum which celebrates the life of Seamus Heaney, who was awarded the Nobel Prize for English Literature in 1995. He was born in Castledawson and his grave is nearby.

The Ghostly Horse Seen Near Benburb

Thank you, Art O'Dailaigh for making the hairs on the back of my neck stand on end by telling me this story!

Art had a friend who was courting a girl from County Armagh. One night, his friend, having taken his girlfriend home, was travelling along the Tullysaran Road near Benburb in his van when he saw a huge black horse standing on the road in front of him. He didn't want to injure it, so he stopped his van, leaving the engine running. The horse walked slowly towards him. It was a bright, moonlit night in spring and he was able to see the animal clearly. Its shoulders were covered in angleberries and there was something strange about it. He realised, to his horror, it was a ghost because there was no sound coming from its hooves as they hit the road.

The horse came up to the van, placed its head on the bonnet, looked in through the windscreen and gazed into Art's friend's eyes. The van's engine stopped. The horse gave the man a penetrating stare, shook its head and disappeared. Art's friend felt shocked and sat very still. He didn't move and was startled when the van's engine started up again by itself.

The next day, Art saw his friend looking very shaken, asked what was wrong and was told about the black horse. His friend said he found it hard to credit what he'd experienced. Other friends were not sympathetic. They said, 'That served you right! You should know better than go out with a girl from County Armagh!'

STONE IN CASTLECAULFIELD THAT WEEPS BLOOD

This is a very sad ghost story. Don't read it if you are feeling in the least depressed.

One of the internal walls of the ancient castle from which Castlecaulfield takes its name has a stone that weeps blood. In the past the daughter of one of the owners of the castle fell in love with someone she considered her knight in shining armour. Her father didn't think his daughter's lover was a sufficiently good match and suspected that she intended to elope, so he imprisoned her within the castle. The knight was killed in battle and the daughter died of a broken heart. Her sorrow was so intense that it seeped into the walls of the castle causing one of its stones to weep blood.

'Will ye luk at yon blood coming out of yon stone!'

HAUNTED BALLYSCULLION HOUSE

Thanks are due to the present owners of Ballyscullion House, near Bellaghy Bawn, for sharing this story with me.

Ballyscullion House is a lovely Georgian house set in beautiful parkland which has provided a setting for the popular television series, *Game of Thrones*. Its present owner says he didn't believe in ghosts until his daughter described a figure she saw in the drawing room of the house dressed in the type of costume worn in the 1920s. Her description fitted that of his grandmother. Several years later he was at a social event where he met a woman, who claimed to be able to communicate with the dead. She told him she saw the spirit of a woman looking over his left shoulder and described his grandmother and what she was wearing accurately. He later had a very similar experience in London, this time with a woman who claimed to be psychic.

THE LONE PIPER OF CASTLEDERG CASTLE

I'd like to thank all the delightful people I met in Castlederg, in the Red Pepper café, a local bar, a community centre and last, but not least, the library.

Castlederg Castle is also known as Davies' Bawn. It was built by Sir John Davies during the Plantation of Ulster and was of great strategic importance because it sits on a commanding site beside the River Derg.

Recent excavations have shown the remains of an earlier fifteenth-century O'Neill Tower House under the bawn. It was the site of many battles sparked by fierce rivalry between the O'Neills and the O'Donnells and later between the native Irish and the settlers. The bawn acted as a place of refuge for planter families during the 1641 rebellion, when it was attacked by Sir Phelim O'Neill and destroyed.

Today the castle ruins consist of the remains of a rectangular bawn. It originally had square flankers at each corner, but the ones by the riverside were washed away when the river flooded. They were originally open-topped to provide a good firing point for artillery. The flankers on the north side of the castle had roofs and formed part of the living area.

In the past people dug tunnels under castles as an escape route if the castle was besieged and attacked. These escape passageways often had several exits and a complicated structure. Long-forgotten passageways exist under Davies' Bawn and are said to be haunted by a lost, lone piper. The bawn is now in ruins and on dark, quiet nights the melancholy strains of the lone piper can be heard coming from far below the ground.

DUGANNON'S GHOSTLY BLACK SERGEANT

The Black Sergeant has been sighted many times stalking the Oaks Road, near Drumglass Hospital, which was once a private house. Its owners were once given police protection and every evening a sergeant and a constable were assigned the duty of guarding it.

One evening the Black Sergeant was sent along with a young constable, who was deeply in love and planning to get married. In those far-off days, employers had what we would consider unreasonable powers. Employees could lose their jobs because they didn't go to church on Sunday, got drunk and so on. If you wanted to get married, you had to ask for your employer's permission! So far the young constable had neglected to ask for that permission.

Now, the Black Sergeant and young constable hated each other and when the sergeant got wind of the constable's plan to marry, out of sheer spite, said he was going to inform their superiors. The constable was very upset. He knew he'd be dismissed if the Black Sergeant carried out his threat. He pleaded for his plans to be kept secret but to no avail. The pair argued and argued. Eventually the constable became enraged, took out his gun and shot the sergeant dead. He was panic-stricken when he realised what he had done, jumped on the back of his horse and attempted to escape. Unfortunately, all Royal Irish Constabulary horses had markings branded on them so he was picked up, tried, found guilty of murder and hanged.

'Stop yer girning! I am going to tell on you.'

The following four ghost stories were told to me by a bartender near Omagh. He made me promise to keep him anonymous because 'There are enough people round here who consider I've lost my marbles without them knowing what I've told you is recorded in a book!' All I can say is, 'Thank you for the craic, the help and for trusting me to keep you anonymous.'

THE WHITE LADY OF SESKINORE

Mary Perry married Alexander McClintock in 1781 and settled in the village of Seskinore. The McClintock family were enthusiastic huntsmen who established the 'Tyrone Hunt'. It was renamed the 'Seskinore Hunt' in 1886.

The daughter of the old castle at Mullaghmore was betrothed to an attractive young sportsman. It was a match based on true love and not a marriage of convenience, as was so often the case in the past. A huge, joyous wedding was arranged with a hunt as part of the festivities. The groom-to-be joined the hunt while his bride donned her wedding gown and prepared for the ceremony. Unfortunately, the young man's horse threw him and he was killed. His bride died from shock and her ghost, dressed in wedding finery, may be seen haunting Cow Lane, which used to be called the Fox Covert, looking for her lost love.

'Don't look now! I think she's after us.'

The courtyard and stable block are all that remain of the old McClintock estate.

OMAGH'S WHITE LADY

The Northern Railway line runs past Loretta Convent in Omagh. There once was a nun who lived in the convent and walked in her sleep. One night, she wandered, while fast asleep, out of the convent and along the railway line, where she was killed by a train. Her ghost, clad in her white nightdress, haunts the line.

THE GHOST THAT PUSHES A PRAM AROUND CLANABOGAN

There was a young woman from Clanabogan who desperately wanted to have a baby. It took her a long time to become pregnant and she was absolutely delighted to find she was expecting. She'd always wanted to

'What's wrong with seeing your woman pushing a pram?' 'She's dead, that's what!'

be a mother and it seemed as if her dreams were about to be realised. Unfortunately, her longed-for baby was born dead. She was so upset she couldn't accept the fact. She put it in a pram and pushed it along the road.

The poor lady didn't live long after that and her ghost has been seen by many, including the bartender's father, pushing her pram along Clonabogan Road.

At this point, by sheer coincidence, a friend of the bartender came into the bar. The bartender said, 'Would ye ever tell this woman about what happened to our fathers as they walked along the Clanabogan Road late one night?' His friend shivered and said. 'Aye. They both saw the ghost of yon poor woman pushing a pram. I'm telling ye, it scared the livin' daylights outta both of them. They never walked that road late at night again!'

GHOSTS IN STRABANE

I stayed in MK Bar Bed & Breakfast in Strabane and had an interesting conversation with a Joan Kelly, who served lovely fresh eggs for breakfast. She told me about the following ghosts. Thank you, Joan.

Strabane's old graveyard is haunted by the ghost of a little girl who died when she was about 7 years of age. Children are the only people who can see her. Adults become aware of her presence when they see, and hear, a child talking to someone who isn't there! Every child who has talked to the ghost describes a little girl of about 7 years of age dressed in Victorian clothes. The ghost is fussy about the kind of child she talks to. She never bothers with confident, rowdy children – just shy, timid ones and she never frightens them. She just sits on the small walls surrounding many graves and chats away. Her last recorded appearance was, according to Joan, about two years ago, in around 2013.

St Ann's Convent in Strabane is very old and it is attached to the local primary school that Joan attended as a child. Joan said she and the children in the school were terrified to go near the long dark

' ... and she walked through the door and it
wasn't open!'

corridors of the old convent because the ghost of a nun, dressed in
white, could be seen walking along them.

THE GHOST WHO HAUNTS BRIAN O'NOLAN'S
(FLANN O'BRIEN) OLD HOME IN STRABANE

*Thanks are due to Nick Kennedy, Strabane Historical Society, for giving
me this story.*

The O'Nolan family once rented a house in Strabane with a garden
out front, a yard behind and a private path leading down through the
fields to the river, which was a great shortcut to town. The house was
haunted by a poltergeist.

The house had originally been a single-storey dwelling consisting
of four rooms before a two-storey extension was built behind it. Brian
and his brothers slept in the front part of the house while his sister
Róisín, who was about 4 years of age at the time, slept in the upstairs
bedrooms.

Shortly after the family moved in, their mother woke during the night and knew something was wrong. She lay listening, wondering what was happening. She heard a window being pulled up roughly and the sound of a small iron ball being rolled along the bedroom floor, followed by something heavy making loud bumps as it fell downstairs. She was very frightened, got out of bed and went to see what had happened. To her surprise, she found all the windows were shut tightly. There was nothing there.

Sometimes strange things happened during the day. Brian's mother occasionally heard a great commotion coming from the kitchen when she was in the living room. It sounded as if a couple of hens had come in and were flying about but there was nothing there when she went to investigate. There weren't even any hens near the door. On other occasions everything on the mantelpiece in the drawing room was thrown on the floor.

A small room near the kitchen had a locked door. The landlord didn't mention it, didn't leave a key and didn't give a reason why it was locked. That room had a barred window high up on the outside wall. When Brian's mother took a kitchen chair outside, stood on it and peered in she saw nothing except from a bare floor and a shelf.

Brian's mother became too frightened to be able to sleep in the house without adult company. Her husband was often away on business so she asked her sister, Theresa, to come and stay with her.

Aunt Theresa usually arrived about eight o'clock every evening and came into the house through the back door. Sometimes steps were heard on the gravel outside and they would assume she had arrived. But then nobody appeared. Half an hour later steps on the gravel would be heard again and Aunt Theresa would appear. It was all very mysterious, frightening and a nuisance! My informant, Nick Kennedy, says since the O'Nolan family left the house there has been no more trouble from the ghost.

A LEGEND OF TYRONE

I found the following verses, by Ellen O'Leary, in Irish Fairy and Folk Tales, *edited by W.B. Yeats. It epitomises Victorian sentimentality over death and would make your glass eye tearful! It also demonstrates the fact that ghosts found in Tyrone are not necessarily harmful. Most simply appear and don't do anything apart from possibly frightening whoever sees them. This ghost is caring and greeted with joy!*

Crouched around a bare hearth in hard, frosty weather,
Three lonely helpless weans cling close together;
Tangled those gold locks, once bonnie and bright –
There's no one to fondle the baby tonight.

'My mammy I want; oh! my mammy I want!'
The big tears stream down with the low wailing chant.
Sweet Eily's slight arms enfold the gold
'Poor weeny Willie, sure mammy is dead –

And daddie is crazy from drinking all day –
Come down, holy angels, and take us away!'
Eily and Eddie keep kissing and crying –
Outside the weird winds are sobbing and sighing.

All in a moment the children are still,
Only quick coo of gladness from Will,
The shieling no longer seems empty or bare,
For, clothed in soft raiment, the mother stands there.

They gather around her, they cling to her dress;
She rains down soft kisses for each shy caress.
The light, loving touch smooths out tangled locks,
And, pressed to her bosom, the baby she rocks.

He lies in his cot, there's a fire on the hearth;
To Eily and Eddy 'tis heaven on earth,
For mother's deft fingers have been everywhere;
She lulls them to rest in the low *suggaun* chair.

They gaze open-eyed, then the eyes gently close,
As petals fold into the heart of a rose,

But ope soon again in awe, love, but no fear,
And fondly they murmur, 'Our mammie is here.'

She lays them down softly, she wraps them around;
They lie in sweet slumbers, she starts at a sound,
The cock crows, and the spirit's away –
The drunkard steals in at the dawning of day.

Again and again, 'twixt dark and the dawn,
Glides in the dead mother to nurse Willie Bawn:
Or is it an angel who sits by the hearth?
An angel in heaven, a mother on earth.

                                        Ellen O'Leary

5

THE PUDDING BEWITCHED

Thanks are due to the late Herbert Bell, the antiquarian book expert, for introducing me to William Carleton's stories and to Dr Eileen Sullivan, Malcolm Duffy, Jack Johnston and the William Carleton Summer School for giving me a greater understanding and appreciation of them. The next four chapters give a flavour of his work. I love the variety of Carleton's tales, from the humour of 'The Pudding Bewitched' to the darkness of the story about 'Leanhaun Shee'. The insight he gives into life during the early part of the nineteenth century and the richness of the characters he writes about are completely fascinating. Every story is different and full of interest.

The language and length of Carleton's stories may cause difficulty for readers today so I have retold a few of my favourite tales and hope you enjoy them as much as I have.

I love the humorous way Carleton begins the story of 'The Pudding Bewitched': 'Moll Roe Rafferty was the son – daughter, I mane, of old Jack Rafferty, who was remarkable for a habit he had of always wearing his head undher his hat: but indeed the same family was a quare one, as everybody knew that was acquainted wid them. It was said of them – but whether it was thrue or not I won't undhertake to say, for afraid I'd tell a lie – but whenever they don't wear shoes or boots they always went barefooted.'

Old Jack Rafferty had two children, a son called Paddy and a daughter called Molly Roe.

Molly Roe was a fine bouncing girl with a shock of flaming red hair that matched her temper. One of the reasons she was called 'Roe' was, according to Carleton, because 'her arms and cheeks were much the colour of her hair, and her saddle nose was the purtiest thing of its kind that ever was on a face'. She had fists with 'a strong simularity to two thumpin' turnips' and 'we have it on good authority there was no danger of their getting blue-moulded for want of use'. 'She had a twist, too, in one of her eyes that was very becomin' in its way' and made her poor husband, when she got him, take it into his head that she could see round a corner.

A vagabond named Gusty Gillespie lived in the neighbourhood and he was 'just as much overburdened with beauty as herself'. 'He was good-looking when seen in the dark' and they became attached to each other during nightly meetings. This was very unfortunate because Molly Roe was a Catholic and Gusty was what was referred to as a 'black-mouth Presbyterian'! The situation caused such a scandal that Molly Roe's brother, Paddy, believed the family honour was being brought into question by the behaviour of the young people. He gave Gusty two choices: marry Molly or else! Gusty knew his man, came to his senses and arranged to be spliced on the following Sunday by the Presbyterian parson, the Rev. Samuel McShuttle.

It had been a long time in the neighbourhood since a black-mouth Presbyterian had married a Catholic and there were strong objections to it from both sides of the community. In fact, the marriage wouldn't have taken place at all if one of the bride's uncles, Harry Connolly, who was a fairy man, hadn't objected. He didn't want to see his niece marry a black-mouth. No way! He did his best to prevent it and got up the noses of Molly's friends to such an extent that they changed their minds and did their best to encourage the match.

When the big day arrived, Molly went to Mass and Gusty to his Presbyterian service, after which the young couple were to join one another in the bride's parents' house. It was arranged for Father McSorley, the priest, to come up after mass to dine with them to keep the officiating clergyman, Mr McShuttle, company. Molly's friends hoped the priest would bless the young couple's union because they didn't trust the kind of marriage McShuttle would give them!

Jack Rafferty and his wife stayed behind to prepare the meal and there was nobody else in the house. Mrs Rafferty was in the process of tying a big bag around a pudding before boiling it in a large pot, when in through the door walked auld Harry Connolly, the fairy man. He was in a rage and shouted, 'BLOOD AND BLUNDERBUSSES, WHAT ARE YEZ HERE FOR?'

'What are ye on about, Harry?'

'Can't you see the sun's in the suds and the moon in high Horlicks. There's a lipstick comin', an' there yez are as unconcerned as if it was about to rain. Go out and cross yerselves three times in the name of the four Mandromarvins, for as the prophecy says, "Fill the pot, Eddy, superbnaculum, a blazing star's an spectaculum. Go out both of you now and look at the sun. Ye'll see the condition he's in.'

Jack bounced towards the door and the pair of them leapt outside like 2-year-olds and jumped upon the stile beside the house to see what was wrong with the sky.

'Jack,' says she, 'do ye see anything wrong?'

'I can't spy anything, sorry, the full of my eye. I can't even see the sun on account of the clouds. I don't think anything's going to happen.'

'Harry knows a lot more than we do. What would put him in such a state barring the threat of a terrible calamity?'

'I doubt it's this marriage, but it can't be helped now. You'll not see a taste of the sun willin' to show his face on it. Just between the two of us, it's not over an' above religious for our Moll til be marrying a black mouth, but as I say it can't be helped. There's nothin' we can do about it.'

His wife winked with both her eyes and said, 'It's enough if Gusty's satisfied with Molly. I know who'll carry the whip hand! In the meantime, let's ask Harry what ails the sun.' They went inside and asked Harry, who screwed up his mouth in a dry smile and replied, 'Ah! The sun has a hard twist of the colic, but don't worry. I tell ye, ye'll have a merrier weddin' than ye think.' And with that he lifted his hat and left the house. The old couple were greatly relieved by Harry's reply so they shouted after him, inviting him to dinner.

The wife finished tying up the pudding, put it into the pot to be boiled and prepared the dinner at the rate of the hunt while Jack sat contentedly smoking his pipe. After a while, he became puzzled by the behaviour of the cooking pot. 'Katty,' says he, 'what the divil do ye have in yon cooking pot? Thunder and sparkles, look at it! It's dancing a jig!'

Katty looked up and, sure enough, there was the pot bobbing up and down, from side to side, jigging away as merry as a grig. It was easy to see it wasn't the pot but whatever was inside it that was causing it to do a hornpipe.

'By the hole of o' my coat,' shouted Jack, 'there's something alive inside thon pot or it would never cut such capers. In the name of all that's holy, what do ye have inside thon puddin'?'

'Begorrah!' cried Katty. 'Something strange has got into it! Wire, man alive, what's to be done?'

As she spoke the pot cut the buckle in fine style and did a spring of which a dancing master would be proud. The lid flew off and out bounced the pudding, which hopped about the floor as nimble as a pea on a drum.

Katty crossed herself and screamed. Jack blessed himself and shouted, 'In the name of all goodness, keep away. No one here will hurt you.' The pudding made a set at him and he leapt first on a chair and then on the table. It then danced towards Katty, who was on her knees, repeating her prayers at the top of her voice. The pudding appeared to be amused by her distress and went hopping and jogging around her.

'If I could get the haul of a pitchfork,' yelled Jack. 'By goxty I'd settle its hash!'

'No! No! NO!' screamed Katty. 'There might be a fairy inside it. Goodness knows what it might do. We should treat it kindly. Pudding dear, please take it easy. Don't harm honest people who never meant to offend you. It wasn't us, troth, it was auld Harry Connolly who bewitched you. Chase him if ye must, but spare a woman like me, for, whisper dear, I'm not in a condition to be frightened.'

The pudding seemed to take her at her word because it danced towards Jack, who, following the example of his wife, also talked nicely to it.

'If it please your honour, my wife only speaks the truth. Upon my voracity we'd both feel much obliged to your honour for being quiet. It's clear: if you weren't a gentlemanly pudding you'd act differently. Auld

Harry, the rogue, is who you should be chasing. He's just gone down the road and if you go quickly you'll be able til catch him. By my song, your dancing master did his duty. Thank you, your honour. God speed you and may you never meet a clergyman nor an alderman in your travels!'

As Jack spoke the pudding hopped out the door and turned down towards the bridge, following in Harry's footsteps. It was only natural for Jack and Katty to follow. It was a Sunday and there were more people than usual on the road. When they saw Jack and Katty following the pudding, their curiosity got the better of them and they ran after it.

'Jack Rafferty, Katty, ahagur, will you tell us, in the name of all that's wonderful, what's going on?'

'Why,' cried Katty, 'it's my big pudding that's been and gone and been bewitched. It's chasing the person that put pishrogues in it!'

Jack's courage came back to him when he realised he had neighbours to help him. 'Katty,' he said, 'you'd better go back home now and make another pudding. Thon big pudding runnin' down the road is no fit til ate. Paddy Scalan's wife, Bridget, says she'll let you boil it on her fire as you'll want ours to cook the rest of the dinner. Paddy's going to lend me his pitchfork. I'll knock the wind out of yon puddin' now I've got the neighbours til back me up.'

Katty went back to finish making the dinner while Jack and half the townland fetched spades, graips, pitchforks, scythes, flails and all manner of other implements to attack the pudding. On and on the pudding went, at a rate of about 6 Irish miles an hour. Such a chase had never been seen – Catholics, Protestants and Presbyterians all after the same pudding. The only thing that could save it was its own activity. People began prodding at it, but it gave a hop here, a skip there, so they missed and hit each other. Big Frank Farrell, the miller of Ballyboulten, got a prod that brought such a hullabaloo out of him you could have hear it at the far end of the parish. Somebody got a whack of a scythe, another a whack of a flail and a third a rap of a spade that made him look nine ways at once!

People were on the point of having a fight when the pudding turned down a wee lane leading to the Methodist preaching house. Immediately everyone began shouting, 'It's a Wesleyan! Come on boys! Where's your pitchforks? Let the wind out of it!' They thought they had trapped it against the side of the church when it gave them the slip, hopped over to the left, jumped into the river and sailed away before their eyes. Colonel Bragshaw had built his demesne wall along each bank of the river so there was no way the crowd could follow the pudding. They went home again, every man, woman and child wondering what had got into the pudding, what it meant and where it was going. If Jack Rafferty and his wife had been willing to say they suspected Harry Connolly had bewitched it there is no doubt that he would have been badly treated by the crowd because their blood was up. However, they had enough sense to keep their suspicions to themselves. Harry was an auld bachelor and a kind friend to the Raffertys. Of course there was a lot of gossip about the pudding, with some guessing this and others guessing that.

In the meantime, Katty went home, prepared another pudding and took it over to her next-door neighbour, Paddy Scalan. It was placed in a pot and set on the fire to boil in the hope that it would be ready in time. They had invited the minister and he loved a warm slice of a good pudding as much as any gentleman living in Europe.

The day passed. Molly and Gusty were made man and wife and couldn't have seemed like a more loving couple. The wedding guests had a pleasant time sauntering around in little groups until dinner time. There was a lot of chatter, laughter and discussion about the behaviour of the pudding as its fame had spread like wildfire throughout the entire parish.

It was near dinner time and Paddy Scalan and his wife Bridget were sitting comfortably beside their fire, watching the pudding boil, when in walked Harry Connolly. He was all in a flutter. 'Blood and blunderbusses what are you here for?'

'Arra, why Harry, why, avick?' gasped Bridget.

'Why, says Harry, 'the sun's in the suds an' the moon in high Horlicks! There's a clipstick comin' on an' there you are, sitting as unconcerned as if it was about to rain the morrow. Go out both of you and look at the sun to see the condition he's in.'

'All right. Harry, but what's that rolled up in the tail of your cothamore?'

'Out with yez,' says Harry, 'and pray against the clipstick – the sky's falling.'

Paddy and his wife were so upset by Harry's wild, piercing eyes that they rushed out the door to see what was making the sky so threatening. They looked in every direction but all they could see was a good-humoured sun beaming down from the sky with not a cloud in sight. They started laughing and went back into the house to scold Harry for teasing them. 'Musha, ye ramscallion ye, Harry …' said Paddy as they were going through the door. No sooner were the words out of his mouth than he met Harry with a wild reek of smoke, like a limekiln, coming out of the tail of his coat.

'Harry!' shouted Bridget. 'By my sowl, the tail of your cothamore's on fire! You'll be burned. Can't you see the smoke coming out of it?'

'Cross yourselves three times,' yelled Harry, without stopping, 'for as the prophecy says, fill the pot …' They could hear no more because Harry had disappeared out of sight. He looked like a man who was carrying something uncomfortably hot, judging by the liveness of his motions and the quare faces he made as he rushed along.

'What the dickens was Harry carrying under his coat?' asked Paddy.

'By my sowl, maybe he's stolen the pudding!' exclaimed Bridget, immediately rushing towards the pot and examining it. The pudding was safe as tuppence, merrily boiling away without a care in the world. The couple were puzzled. What did Harry have under his coat? What had he done when they were sky-gazing? What was he up to?'

The day passed, the dinner was ready and a fine crowd gathered to partake of it. The Presbyterian minister met the Methodist preacher as he walked up the road leading to Jack Rafferty's and insisted on him coming along to join the feast – and a devilish stretch of an appetite he had in truth! In those days, clergy of all descriptions were the best of friends.

They had nearly finished their dinner when Jack Rafferty asked for a slice of pudding. Just as he spoke Bridget carried it in through the door. It was huge – as big as a mess pot!

'Gentlemen,' said Harry, 'I hope none of you will refuse a bit of Katty's pudding. I don't mean the one that went that took to its travels today by dancing round the roads. I mean the good solid fellow she made since then.'

'To be sure we won't,' replied the priest, 'so Jack, just put a good slice of pud on the three plates at your right hand and send them over here to the clergy, but maybe, Jack, we won't show a good example!'

'With a heart and a half, yer reverence, in troth it's not a bad example any of ye ever set. I just wish I'd better food to set in front of you. We're poor people so you can't expect to get what you would in better places.'

'Better a meal of herb where peace is ...' replied the Methodist preacher before stopping in amazement as the priest and the minister jumped up from the table and began dancing a lively jig.

At this moment a neighbour's son came running in to tell them that the parson was coming to see the newlyweds and wish them happiness. The words were hardly out of his mouth when the parson appeared in the doorway and stopped in amazement at the sight of the minister footing it away at a rate of knots. He hadn't time to sit down before the Methodist preacher jumped up and started clapping his two fists at his sides in great style.

'Jack Rafferty,' he exclaimed, 'what's the meaning of this?'

'I can't say, but will your reverence taste a morsel of this pudding so the young couple can boast you attended their wedding.'

'Well,' says he, 'I will, just to gratify them, so just a morsel.' He put a spoonful in his mouth and exclaimed, 'Jack, this bates Banagher! Have you a spot of the cratur til go along with it?'

'I sure have. There's always plenty of drink in this house.'

He had scarcely got the words out of his mouth when the parson, who was an active man, cut a caper a yard high and all three clergy were dancing as if determined to win a wager. It is impossible to describe the state of the gathering. Some turned their eyes up in wonder, others were hoarse with laughter, while a few thought the clergy had acted high and mighty a trifle too much!

'Begorrah!' exclaimed one, 'Sure it's a crying shame til see three black-mouthed preachers in such a state at this early hour! By thunder, I wonder what's come over them. You'd think they were bewitched! Holy Moses, look at the caper the Methodist cuts! As for the rector, who would think he could handle his feet at such a rate! He cuts the buckle equal to Paddy Horaghan, the dancing master himself! Bad cess to the morsel of a parson that's not hard at it, an' it a Sunday too! Whirro, gentlemen, if it's a fun year ye'r after, the more power til yez!'

All of a sudden Jack Rafferty himself was bouncing among them and footing it away like the best of them. No play could equal it and nothing could be heard but laughing, shouts of encouragement and hands clapping like mad. The minute Jack Rafferty had stopped carving the pudding and left his chair auld Harry Connolly had clapped himself down, began carving away and handing out generous slices of pudding and who came in the door but Barney Hartigan, the piper. 'Begorrah,' said Barney, 'you're early at the work, gentlemen. But devil may care, yez shan't feel the want the music while there's a blast in me pipes.' And in his best style, he played 'Jig Polthogue' and 'Kiss My Lady'.

The fun went on thick and threefold while Harry, the auld knave, served the pudding in double quick time. He gave a slice to the bride, who, before you could say 'chopstick', was dancing away with the Methodist preacher, who gave such a jolly spring in front of her that it threw everyone into convulsions. Harry found partners for everybody by sending the pudding round like lightning so, to cut a long story short, there wasn't a pair of heels that wasn't busy dancing as if their lives depended on it.

'Barney,' says Harry, 'this is a bully of a pudding. You've never tasted the like. Try a slice of it. It's beautiful.'

'To be sure, I will,' says Barney, 'but Harry, be quick because my hands are engaged and it would be a thousand pities not to keep the music going with them so well inclined. Thank you, Harry. Begad, this is a famous pudding. Blood and turnips, what's happening?' He bounced up, pipes and all, dashed into the middle of the crowd and shouted, 'Come on ye boyos! Let's make a night of it! The Ballyboulteen boys forever! Come on, yer reverence, heel, toe! Good! Here's for Ballyboulteen and the sky over it!'

The worst was yet to come because when they were in the heat of the dance another pudding came in the door. It was as nimble and merry as the first. It scared the living daylights out of everybody. The three clergy danced out the door, followed by all the wedding guests. The bride and groom danced off to bed. Nobody could break step. It would have made a cat laugh to see the parson dance down the road with the Presbyterian minister and the Methodist preacher cutting the buckle in the opposite direction.

William Carleton said he thought Harry was hand in glove with the good people and got them to put a spell on the pudding. He waited for it when it floated down the river as light as an eggshell. He picked it

'Come on, shake a leg.'

up a couple of miles past the wall around Squire Bradshaw's demesne. The water had washed it as clean as a new pin so he tucked it into the tail of his coat and changed puddings when Paddy Scanlan and his wife were examining the sky. Somehow he managed to bewitch the other pudding in the same manner as the first by getting a fairy to go into it. Some people say auld Harry put half a pound of quicksilver into the pudding, but Carleton said that didn't make sense!

6

THE LEANHAUN SHEE

When I first read this story I didn't like it one little bit! Its blackness made me shudder, then I realised it is a wonderful reflection of the age in which Carleton lived, an age when people, who professed to be Christians, were bogged down in superstitious belief. And who can blame them? Science was undeveloped, the germ theory of disease did not exist, there was no scientific explanation of weather patterns and people sickened and died without apparent reason, as did animals and crops. In these circumstances it was easy to blame misfortune on supernatural forces, such as fairies and witches. The peasantry, like their counterparts throughout Europe, were illiterate. They were ruled by landlords and the Church had a strong hold on them, preaching, as they did, about sin, death and hellfire! Few people dared to question the actions of the clergy, but Carleton did. He was born a Roman Catholic, but he grew disillusioned by the Catholic Church's treatment of starving peasants. He became a Protestant, but he grew disillusioned once more and professed to be an atheist. However, he returned to the Roman Catholic faith before he died. By that time, he had probably gained sufficient wisdom to give clergymen a fool's pardon, realising they are similar to the general population: there are good ones and bad ones and we all fall for temptation.

I admit this story has left me confused because its description of a Leanhaun Shee differs from that of W.B. Yeats. He described a Leanhaun Shee as a beautiful fairy woman, who wandered around the countryside, tempting men to seduce her. If she succeeded with a man, he fell under her power and grew thinner and thinner until eventually he died, unable to find peace even after death. He was doomed to spend eternity as a lonely wandering ghost, but the Leanhaun Shee did, at least, inspire him to write beautiful poetry.

Mary Sullivan was the wife of a wealthy farmer and the niece of the Rev. Felix O'Rourke. Her kitchen was large, comfortable and warm. Her usual garb consisted of a scapular with the dust of a four-leafed clover sewn into its folds so she could see fairies if they happened to be about. When she stood at the sink, there was, to the right, a spotlessly clean salt box and, to her left, a jamb wall, which kept the draught from the door out of the kitchen. The jamb wall had a tiny, pane-less, gothic window to let light in and to enable anyone sitting by the fire to see approaching visitors. The door had two horseshoes (they had been found by accident) hanging above it to bring luck to the household. A bottle of holy water was placed in a little 'hole' in the wall below the salt box to keep the house purified and it had a bunch of fairy flax lying on top of it. A large lump of houseleek grew outside on the copestone of the gable to prevent the house from going on fire and to be used as a cure for sore eyes.

On Palm Sunday, Mary Sullivan had asked the priest to consecrate palm leaves, which she brought home and hung over all the beds in the house and over the cattle in the outhouses. When the cows were about to calf, she wove a silken thread into their tails to keep them from being overlooked (elf-shot) by fairies as they gave birth because she believed fairies had a peculiar power over females. She grew a lot of disease-curing herbs in her garden and had numerous charms to cure headaches, toothaches, colic, warts and other diseases. She had a potion made up by the herb doctor which both she and her husband drank to prevent the slightest misunderstanding between a husband and wife. It was very expensive. The herb doctor had disappeared from the neighbourhood soon after selling it to avoid Mary's husband, Bartley, who said it 'had no effect on Mary, at all, at all, at all!' Mary said as far as the potion was concerned it had worked on her, 'but Bartley was worse than ever after taking it'.

One fine summer evening she was sitting by the fire, knitting a pair of socks for her husband when she felt alarmed, stopped knitting and listened intently as she peered around the hearth. There was no doubt about it: the crickets were back! (Crickets were believed to bring luck to all households that took care of them, but – and it was a serious but – they could bring bad luck if annoyed!)

Mary crossed herself and gasped, 'Queen of saints about us! It's back ye are! Sure you're very welcome. I hope that unlike yer last visit yez are bringing luck now. Our cow died after yer last visit. Here's bread and salt and meal for ye, ye craturs ye!'

She sprinkled a little holy water around the hearth and muttered an Irish prayer to protect her household against the evil crickets can bring.

'There now, ye wee dears,' she said. 'Ye can't say ye were ever mistreated or mocked in this house. Yez have been given a right mouthful of grub and haven't any reason to destroy my best clothes the way you did on yer last visit. I don't think I deserved to have my long stuff body riddled with holes just because that young rascal of a son of mine told yez, in a joke, til clear off. Sure he's just a wee ramscallion. Yez shouldn't have paid any attention til him. He was only having a bit of fun. He didn't mean it.'

At that moment the small window in the jamb wall darkened as a tall women came into the cottage. Mary looked at her and said, 'May the blessing of God be upon ye.'

The woman didn't reply. She looked as if she was in anguish. Her dark eyes appeared wild and tortured. She turned her face to look over her left shoulder as if there was some invisible being following her. 'Hush! Hush! I will do it. I will, I will, I will. Be quiet, will ye! I've told ye I'll do it!'

Mary looked at her and repeated, 'May the blessing of God be upon ye, honest woman. Now if it was cold I'd ask ye til draw a chair up til the fire, but sit down anyway and make yoursel' comfortable.'

The strange woman's piercing eyes glared at her. 'Hush! Hush!' she cried. 'I've told ye I will say it til her. Mary Sullivan, I know ye well. Hush! Hush! I know the power of the thing ye'd carry about ye, if ye had the sense. Ah! Ah! AH! What's this?' she exclaimed loudly before uttering three ear-splitting shrieks that suggested she was in agony.

'In the name of goodness, what's wrong?' exclaimed Mary as she started up from her chair. 'Are you sick?'

The woman's face appeared haggard and distorted. 'Sick?' she gasped, licking her parched lips. 'Sick? Look at this.' She shuddered as she pointed at a huge lump coming up from her left shoulder and covered by a loosely pinned red cloak. 'Here! Look at this!'

'Blessed Mother', exclaimed Mary. 'Today's Friday! Protect me from harm.'

'Ay,' said the stranger. 'Hush, I say, hush. I will say it to her. Ay, indeed! Mary Sullivan, it's with me all the time.'

Mary grabbed the holy water and sprinkled it generously all over herself. 'Blessed Mother,' she yelled, 'the Leanhaun Shee!' She was terrified as she moved towards the strange woman, meaning to throw holy water round her.

'Don't! Don't! Don't!' shrieked the woman. 'Do you want to give me more pain without keeping yourself any safer. It doesn't care about yer holy water but I'd suffer for it and ye might suffer too!'

'Don't,' groaned Mary. 'Good woman, don't come near me for the sake of all the saints and angels in heaven, don't. And what are ye? And how did ye get that thing ye carry with ye?'

'Ye're not doing right asking me that question. It's one that should never cross yer lips. Look til yersel' and what's over ye.'

Mary almost leapt off her seat in terror as she tried to see if her shape had changed. Had she grown a dreadful hump like the stranger? Her hair felt as if it was standing on end as she said, 'Decent woman, sure it's no wonder I asked ye a question because I'm worried about having a Leanhaun Shee under my roof. It's only natural that I should be anxious and curious. I've never seen anyone that looked as wild and tormented as you.'

'Gracious woman,' said the stranger, 'you've been kind to me. I wander the roads and most people hide when they see me coming. I hunger; no one gives me food. I die of thirst, yet no one gives me a sip of water. I want to bring you luck, take this bottle and drink the contents and you'll gain untold wealth.'

Mary looked at the woman with a mixture of fear and greed. She had heard the Leanhaun Shee had the ability to bring luck and wealth, if she chose to do so. She looked around her comfortable kitchen. 'God has been very good to us,' she whispered, 'but of course I could put more wealth to good use, but no! NO! I will not sell my soul to Satan. I don't want to suffer the fires of eternal damnation!'

The Leanhaun Shee uttered oaths of the most serious kind. 'I swear,' she said, 'this little bottle will do you no harm. For my sake, and your own sake, drink it. It will bring untold wealth, to you, and to all those belonging to you. You must stand up as you drink it. Drink half of it at a time, with your face to the east in the morning at sunrise and to the west at night when the sun goes down. Promise me you'll do that.'

'How would drinking that bring me wealth?'

'It's very complicated. I can't tell you. I don't understand it and even if I did I wouldn't tell you. All I can say is you'll feel the effects after you've done what I told you.'

'Keep yer bottle, decent woman. I want no truck with the devil. May the saints above keep me from temptation, which I feel is growing stronger every moment, God above! What's coming over me? I've never in all my life had such a hankering after money! Decent woman, I don't like asking anyone who's had bread at my hearth to leave, but if you go I'll make it worth your while.'

'Take it. Please take it. I swear it'll do you no harm. Please believe me. If you take it, you'll release me from my suffering.'

'No! No! No!' cried Mary. 'Not one drop'll pass my lips, should it make me as wealthy as auld Henderson, who's so stinkin' rich he airs his golden guineas in the sun for fear of them becoming light because they've been lyin' in the dark. Allowing you to make me wealthy isn't a proper way to get money. I won't take it.' With that she sat down very firmly by the fire.

The poor woman cried, 'Am I doomed never to meet anyone who'll take the promise off me by drinking from this bottle? Oh! I'm unhappy. If only I'd kept His commandments when I was young ... I wouldn't now ... Merciful Mother, is there no relief? Torment, kill me outright. Surely the pangs of eternity can't be greater than what I'm suffering now? Mary Sullivan ... your daughters ... teach them ... teach them to ...' Having got so far she stopped, appeared to be shaken by convulsions and a white froth foamed at her mouth. Then she stopped and an awful calmness settled on her as she appeared to glide past the jamb wall and out the door, leaving Mary very shaken, sitting by the fire.

Shortly afterwards, the family returned. Mary's husband, Bartley, was the first one back. He was followed by the three daughters, who'd been milking the cows. The servants dropped in one by one after they had finished their day's work. They placed themselves around the table. Bartley sat in his usual seat, at the head, but Mary didn't join them. She stayed by the fire, looking very upset. She kept crossing herself every few minutes and muttering prayers against evil spirits.

'Why don't ye come til the table while the sowans are still warm?' asked Bartley.

Mary didn't pay any attention until he repeated the question four times and asked, 'Why then, Mary, what's wrong with ye? What's come over you? Are you ill?'

'Supper!' she exclaimed. 'Ill? It's every right I have til be ill. I just hope nothing bad happens. Feel my face. It's as cold and wet as limestone, aye. If you found I was a corpse it wouldn't be at all strange!'

Bartley left the table and went over to the fire. 'Mary dear, turn your face towards the firelight. Why, in the name of all wonder, what ails ye? Ye look like a corpse, sure enough! What happened to put you in such a state? The cold sweat's teemin' off you!'

Mary was so shocked by the stranger's visit that she felt herself becoming weaker and weaker. She asked for a drink of water, but before it could be given to her she fainted. Her family were very upset and became panic-stricken, running hither and thither without really helping. She came round after a few minutes and they realised she was not dead. 'Did you see a strange woman leaving the house?' she asked.

They hadn't seen anyone. 'Bartley, whisper,' she said, beckoning him over to her and in a few words told him about her visitor. He went very pale, crossed himself and exclaimed, 'Mother of Saints! Childer, a Leanhaun Shee! A Leanhaun Shee!' they cried, immediately blessing themselves. 'A Leanhaun Shee! This day's Friday! God protect us from harm!' They listened as Mary described in detail what had happened. Every hair on every head felt as if it was standing on end. Bartley looked soberly into the fire until the cat started prowling round the dresser and knocked a bowl, prompting him to scream, an action immediately copied by everyone in the room.

The next day the story spread throughout the neighbourhood and it didn't lose any horror in the telling. Families who had forgotten to keep supplies of holy water borrowed some from their neighbours and every prayer that had become rusty from lack of use was brushed up. Charms were hung around the necks of cattle and copies of the gospels around the necks of children. Crosses were placed over doors and windows and people made sure not to throw dirty water out before sunrise or after dusk in case they annoyed the fairies.

The woman who had caused such trouble in the parish was pitied, avoided and feared. Nobody knew how she lived because people where too frightened to help her. It was said she existed without meat or drink, doomed to remain alive until she could find somebody weak enough to drink the hellish liquid she carried, which, they said, would cause that person to change places with her.

A man, called Stephenson, had committed suicide on his farm about six months before her appearance. He had lived a lonely, solitary life. He was the only surviving member of his family and he'd never married. Eventually he'd gone mad and hanged himself by a halter from the rafters of his stable. His house was locked up and people said the devil came in every night and repeated the sin by hanging Stephenson from the rafters. The strange woman went to live in Stephenson's old house and people told stories about the horrible things they imagined happened there each night. As the stories circulated, the woman became a greater and greater object of fear. Nobody dared to try help her or send her away because they thought she possessed the terrible powers of a Leanhaun Shee.

Bartley, along with many other people living in the parish, went to Father O'Rourke and asked him to do something about the Leanhaun Shee. Father O'Rouke showed what was considered to be the white feather. Bartley couldn't coax him into agreeing to go and see Mary, even though she hadn't been the same woman since the fateful visit, so he went to see Father Phillip O'Dallaghy. He was a suspended parish priest, a good man who supported himself by attempting to cure people who were ill. He lived a simple life without luxury, any sort of comfort or alcohol.

After Bartley and his friends left Father O'Dallaghy, he looked worried and paced around his room. He began talking to himself, 'Ay,' he said, 'stupid peasants sunk in superstition and ignorance. Maybe you are happier than someone who can only look back on a life full of crime and misery.'

Bartley went home and told his wife that Father Philip O'Dallaghy would call on her the next day to hear her version of the Leanhaun Shee's visit. 'That's good,' she said. 'I intended to go to him anyway to get my new scapular consecrated. And I'll tell you what I'll do. I'll get a set of the gospels for the boys and girls and he can consecrate them when he's at it. They say that man's so holy he can do anything, even melt a body off the face of the earth like snow off a ditch. There's no doubt it's the strange power he has.'

'Well! Ye needn't be gettin' anything in for him to eat or drink. He wouldn't take a glass of whiskey once in seven years. Don't let on, but I think he's a bit too dry. He might be holy enough but able to take an odd sup sometimes. I'd prefer Father Felix O'Rouke. He's much more friendly and he never refuses a glass in reason, although we all know he's not near as holy as Father Philip O'Dallaghy.'

'Do ye know what I was told about Father O'Dallaghy?'

'I don't know, Mary. You tell me, then I'll tell you if I know it after I hear it!'

'Quit yer jokin', Bartley! Ye know Father O'Dallaghy went on a seven-week fast at Lent. His housekeeper and servants were wild worried about him and watched him very carefully. When he was fast asleep they saw a small silk thread come down from the ceiling and enter his mouth. He sucked away at it like a wean at its mother's breast. He was being supported by angels, so he was.'

It was generally known that Father O'Dallaghy was going to visit Mary to hear about the Leanhaun Shee and a lot of parishioners gathered around her house so they'd know what was going on. As the priest approached the house, people who were standing outside fell to their knees, uncovered their heads with one accord and asked his blessing. Father O'Dallaghy looked haggard, as if he hadn't slept well. When he saw the people kneel, he shook his hand over them and muttered some words that seemed more like a mockery of the ceremony than anything else. The people arose, dusted their knees, put on their hats and looked as if they felt better.

When he entered the house, Mary gave him her best chair, stirred the fire and a space was cleared around him to show respect.

'My dear neighbour,' he said, 'I'm told you had a visit from a strange woman. What has got you in such a state? Now please sit down.'

'I can't credit it, indeed an' sowl!'

'I humbly thank Your Reverence,' said Mary as she gave a low curtsey. 'I'd rather not sit. I know what respect means, Your Reverence.'

'About this woman, this Leanhaun Shee,' said the priest, 'what precisely do you mean by a Leanhaun Shee?'

'Why, sir, some strange bein' from the fairies that sticks to some people. There's a bargain, Your Reverence, between them, and the devil, who, saints about us, has had a hand in it. If the bargain is broken, the devil has the person in his power. The only way to get rid of a Leanhaun Shee is to get someone else to take your place. The Leanhaun Shee has the power to bring you untold riches, but what use is that to you if you lose your place in the eternal kingdom? But sure, Your Reverence, what call do I have telling you about Leanhaun Shees. Sure, you must know all about them.'

Father O'Dallaghy gave his usual peculiar smile and started to ask more questions about Mary's strange visitor when there was a commotion outside. 'Please, sir, they're comin'! They're comin' this very moment! THEY'RE COMIN'!'

'Who are coming?' asked Father O'Dallaghy in a supercilious tone.

'Why, the woman, sir, and her good pet, the Leanhaun Shee.'

'Why are you making such a fuss? Let her come in and we'll see just how capable she is of injuring her fellow man. It's probably some maniac ...' and he started to talk to himself in a very low voice nobody could hear.

'He's saying a prayer now,' said one of the crowd. 'Haven't we a good right to be thankful he's in the place with us or goodness knows what harm'd be done.'

'Look! Look! Look! It's Father O'Rourke. He's coming too!'

The terrible woman came into the room and looked startled to see so many people standing there. She was still carrying the dreadful hump on her back. She stood still for at least two minutes during which time you could have heard a feather drop. Nobody spoke. The crowd looked terrified. The poor woman's breath was thought to carry disease and her touch to cause paralysis.

'Please, Your Reverence, that's her,' said Bartley pointing towards her as he spoke. He avoided looking directly at her in case he was given the evil eye.

Father O'Dallaghy arose, walked forward a few steps and confronted her. 'Woman,' he said sternly, 'tell me who you are, what you are and why you have assumed a character of such a repulsive nature.'

The tall figure stood before him. The silence was deafening, every breath was hushed, no one moved. It was as if the room was filled with statues. The heaving of the woman's breast showed she was undergoing some sort of terrible internal struggle. Her face became even paler, her lips turned blue and her eyes burned like coals of fire in her head.

'Speak!' demanded Father O'Dallaghy.

The woman appeared to be gathering strength. She became composed as she uncovered the part of her dress that partially hid her face.

'Who and what am I?' she asked. 'I am the victim of your infidelity. Thanks to you I am scoffed and scorned by the world, freezing in winter, scorched by summer's heat, withered by starvation, hated by man. I have no rest. I am haunted by guilt. I am the unclean spirit who can't find rest. Look! This failed!' she held out the bottle of water. 'I live to accuse you. You are my husband, although our union was a guilty one. You flew to avoid punishment, but the finger of God is pointed at you. I am what you made me. And you,' she continued, turning towards Mary, 'you good woman, you were kind to me. I came to apologise for frightening you and to beg a little bread. I have not eaten for three days. There is nothing in this bottle but water. There is nothing in it to harm you. This hump on my back is nothing more than the robe I wore when I was an innocent in my peaceful convent.'

Father O'Dallaghy looked around. Every eye was on him. At last he spoke. 'You poor wretches should put confidence in God, not frail man. That way you'll not be leaning on a broken reed.'

'Father O'Rourke, you have been a witness of my disgrace, but not my punishment. I have been wracked with guilt. I cannot find peace.'

'Come, Margaret, come with me. I can give you shelter, food, drink, but no peace. No peace!'

He took her by the hand and led her to his home. He seemed distracted. His blood appeared to have turned to fire. He paced up and down in his room and demanded a large fire be built. The Almighty's vengeance caught his imagination. Was he damned? He heard voices and ran out of the house and up into the glen where he looked at its picturesque meanders, tall trees, wild underwood and grey rocks mellowed by the moonlight. He tried to remember what had happened the previous day but it was wiped from his memory. The voice of his conscience thundered in his head. He felt he was being pursued by fiends. He rushed back into the house, tearing his hair out. He caught sight of himself in the looking glass. His hair had turned pure white. He looked at the fire. 'Ah!' he cried. 'I see the light. I see hope. I will sacrifice my material body in the fire to save my soul from the eternal fires of hell.' Next day he was found, burnt to a cinder, all except his feet and legs. His razor and several clots of gore were found around the hearth. He had cut himself so he became so weak because of loss of blood that he could not crawl out of the fire, even if he'd wished to escape such a terrible death. As for the Leanhaun Shee, she lived for several more years, wandering around the countryside, living in scalpeens, hated and feared by all.

7

A LEGEND OF
KNOCKMANY

This is one of my favourite stories. I love telling it to children because of how they usually react to a giant climbing into a cradle and I think Oonagh is a great role model for girls.

Knockmany, in the Clogher Valley, is also known as Baine's Hill, the hill of the monks, or as Anya's Cove locally.

Finn started to build the Giant's Causeway because he wanted to cross the Irish Sea to knock the melt out of a Scottish giant, who was very annoying. He kept shouting abuse at Finn and no self-respecting giant can tolerate that. He was working away when he heard that the great giant Cúchulainn, the champion of Ulster, was coming up from County Louth to fight him. That was very worrying so he did what a lot of men do when they're worried: he ran home to his wife.

Oonagh was sitting quietly by the fire, nursing their baby, when Finn burst through the door. 'Oonagh,' he gasped, 'I'm in dead trouble. That pesky giant Cúchulainn's coming north to fight me. He's even bigger than I am. I'll be a laughing stock if he knocks the stuffing out of me.'

'Never fash yersel',' replied Oonagh, going over to the door and looking towards the south. She was gifted with amazing vision. She could see the grass grow. She looked south, turned towards Finn and said, 'Yes, I see him. He's striding across the mountains in his seven-league boots. But don't worry, we've got plenty of time to prepare. Now, you dress yourself in the baby's clothes and climb into the cradle.'

'B-b-b-but,' stuttered Finn.

'Never mind the buts! Just you do as you're told and leave the rest to me.'

Oonagh immediately got a blanket and flapped it over the fire like Native Americans do to send smoke signal messages. She asked her sister, who lived on the mountain opposite, to come over, lend her a keg of butter and take the baby out for the rest of the day. Her sister was over in a trice. She brought the butter and carried the baby away.

Oonagh looked at Finn. 'You're a big baby. Look at the cut of ye. Ye can't even put a nappy on tidily!' She adjusted Finn's clothes, tucked him up in the cradle and started to bake scones in her pot oven. She made a normal scone batter and put stones inside half of them. When they were cooked, she laid them carefully along the hearth on a hardening stand to dry. She had just finished when Cúchulainn walked in the door.

'You might have knocked,' snarled Oonagh. 'You near scared the wits out of me.'

'I have come to fight your husband.'

Oonagh smiled. 'I'm glad to hear it. I'm fed up with him. He spends all his time working on the Giant's Causeway and never thinks of coming home and doing a hand's turn around the house or farm. I have to cope all on my own. It's not fair, so it's not. A good thrashing would do him a world of good. It might knock a bit of sense into him. He's out now but I'm expecting him back shortly. Why don't you make yourself comfortable? Sit down and wait for him and I'll give you a wee cup of tea in your hand.'

Cúchulainn sat down on a creepy stool while Oonagh poured some tea out of the kettle that was hanging over the crook and crane, buttered a couple of scones with stones inside them and handed them to Cúchulainn. He took a bite, broke a tooth and let a loud roar, 'Missus dear, why did you give me a scone with a stone inside it?'

'I always put stones inside my scones. It's the only way I can satisfy Finn's appetite. Look how the baby loves them.' Oonagh buttered a couple more scones – the ones without stones – and gave them to the 'baby', who devoured them in a couple of bites.

'That's some baby!' said Cúchulainn.

'Yes,' replied Oonagh. 'The wee dear! He's the spitting image of Finn, so he is.'

Cúchulainn looked thoughtful as he ate three more scones, taking care not to break any more teeth. He went over to the cradle and stood gazing at the 'baby'. 'Yon wean's some size!' he exclaimed.

'I'm glad to hear you say that. His granny says he's small, only half the size Finn was at the same age. Would you do me a favour now you're on yer feet? Would you ever the house round to face the sun? Winter's coming and I believe we should get every glimpse of the sun possible. Finn turns the house away from the sun every summer so it doesn't overheat. He's very thoughtful is my Finn, when he's at home. I'm quare and cauld and would be grateful if you'd move it towards the sun to warm me – that is, if you can do such a thing. You're so much smaller than Finn you might find it difficult.'

Cúchulainn could not face the possibility of being thought weaker than Finn McCool. He went outside, put his arms around the house and pushed and heaved until he got it into the right position. He looked visibly tired as he turned towards Oonagh and said, 'Thank you very much for your hospitality. I'd better go now. I'm expected back home in Dún Dealgan for dinner. Tell your husband I'm sorry to have missed him.' With that, he stretched his legs in his seven-league boots and strode back down south. He was never seen again anywhere near the Clogher Valley and Finn McCool was able to return to building the Giant's Causeway.

8

NEAL MALONE

As someone who is small in stature, I have a certain amount of sympathy for Neal Malone. There is a tendency not to take small people, especially women, seriously and that can be very annoying. Of course it can also be an advantage, as I found when, as a teacher, I saw two senior boys knocking the melt out of each other in a corridor. Without thinking, I got between them and started pushing them apart. They burst out laughing. One of them said, 'Miss, you're awful wee!' The other one said, 'Why don't you jump in the air and kick us on the kneecaps?' I couldn't help laughing and the situation was diffused, but if I'd been Neal Malone I'd have felt humiliated and annoyed.

Neal Malone, the tailor, was 4 feet 4 inches in height (133 centimetres), but although he was no bigger than a sparrow's fart, he had the fighting soul of a champion. He had been born into a famous fighting family. His father, grandfather and great-grandfather were all fighting men and they were, in all probability, descended from Con of the Hundred Battles himself.

Neal strode around the world with great confidence, looking for someone to fight. He always carried a cudgel but he could never find an opponent. Nobody would fight him because of his small stature. He did his best by challenging all the pugilists of the parish, even attempting to provoke 14-stone men, but to no avail. They just laughed and said, 'You're only wee. Away and fight someone your own size!' It was very annoying.

'Blur-an-agers!' he exclaimed one day when he was half tipsy at the fair. 'Am I never to get a bit of fightin'? Is there no cowardly spalpeen fit to stand before Neal Malone? The life I'm leadin' is a disgrace to my relations and to my ancestors. I'm blue-moulded for want of a batin'! Will nobody fight me for love, money or whiskey? Friend or foe, I don't care who it is. Will somebody, for friendship's sake, join me in a bit of a punch-up?'

Neal did everything he could to provoke a fight. He insulted and abused all his acquaintances, did everything he could think of to be annoying and told lies that would have choked an elephant and made a novelist blush and feel they lacked imagination. He felt it was a terrible tragedy not to have a single enemy. It was a crying shame, as far as he was concerned, that in his presence the world became astonishingly Christian. Anyone he struck on the cheek simply turned the other one! What use was it carrying his cudgel everywhere he went? Why, when he knit his brows and shook his kippeen at his fiercest friends they just laughed. His appearance was a signal for peace, no matter how much he wanted warfare.

Eventually Neal became so upset it affected his work as a tailor. He sat cross-legged, in the manner of all tailors, and worried. He brandished scissors at clients in a threatening fashion. He wasted a lot of chalk by marking cloth in the wrong places and, horror of horrors, he even caught his hot goose without a holder and burnt his hands! His friends became very worried and persuaded him to visit a doctor, which is something Tyrone folk are reluctant to do. Eventually he agreed and went to please them, but it didn't matter what medicine he was given, it didn't cure his disease. He still wanted to fight! Then the doctor recommended bloodletting. Neal considered that an insult! He was convinced that to lose blood in a peaceful manner was not only cowardly, but a bad cure for courage. He would have none of it. It would be sacrilege to lose his fighting blood like that! His relatives bled during, and after, fighting. He was not going to be a disgrace to his name by losing blood meekly to a doctor with a lancet! No way! His blood was reserved for heroic purposes!

He decided the doctor was useless and became depressed, although his friends did their best to cheer him up. 'Keep yer pecker up!' they suggested. 'We'll do our best to get you a couple of enemies, you'll see.' That promise worked for a little while but as day after day passed without the possibility of getting into a scrap, he decided his heroic soul was decaying for lack of use. He looked at his scissors and the point of his needle bitterly as he thought of his spirit lying rusting inside him. He decided to fight his own shadow. It refused to fight in any position other than with its back to a wall. One day he went out into the garden at midday and his shadow looked ready for a proper fight, but a cloud gave it an opportunity to disappear. Neal saw that fate was against him and sank into a deep depression. He lost his health, spirits, bluster – everything except his courage. He became thinner and thinner and had to take his clothes in several times. It's hard to believe he was reduced to skin and bone by friendship, although it's true that more people have risen in the world because of the actions of their enemies than those of their friends.

One day Neal was sitting cross-legged, as usual, while pressing a pair of inexpressibles. He stopped and sat still, with his hands on the handle of his goose and his chin resting on the back of his hands. He was the picture of misery when Mr O'Connor, the schoolmaster, came into his workshop to collect his inexpressibles. He was having them turned for the third time.

'Mr O'Connor,' said the tailor, 'will you please sit down?'

Mr O'Connor sat down, put his hat on his knee, his half-hand-kerchief in his pocket and looked at the tailor. The tailor looked at Mr O'Connor and neither of them spoke for several moments. Neal was wrapped up in his own misery while Mr O'Connor was wrapped in his. Neal gazed at Mr O'Connor and felt sympathy as he became aware of his friend's misery. Mr O'Connor gazed at the tailor, saw how unhappy he was and was upset by his friend's misery. At last he spoke. 'Neal, are my inexpressibles finished?'

'I'm in the process of ironing them, but by my sowl it's not your inexpressibles I'm thinkin' about. I'm not a ninth part of the man I was. I can hardly make a collar now.'

'Neal, are you still able to carry a staff?'

'I've a light hazel one that's quare and handy, but what's the use of carrying it when I can't get anyone who'll fight with me? Sure, I'm disgracing my relatives by the life I'm leadin'! I'll go to the grave without every batin' a man or bein' batin' myself. Devil the row have I ever been able to drum up in my life. I'm blue-moulded for want of a batin'. But if you have patience ...'

'Patience!' exclaimed Mr O'Connor with a sad shake of his head, 'Patience? Did I hear you say "patience"?'

'Ay, an' by my sowl, if you deny I said "patience" I'll bate your head in.'

'Ah Neal,' sighed the schoolmaster, 'I don't deny it, though I'm teaching mathematics, philosophy and knowledge every day of my life, yet I'm learning patience day and night. I've forgotten how to deny anything. I haven't contradicted anything outside school hours for fourteen years. About twelve years ago, I expressed a shadow of doubt, but now I've even stopped doubting. That last doubt was my final attempt to maintain domestic authority in my own home and I suffered for it.'

'Well,' said Neal, 'if you have patience I'll tell you what's bothering me from beginning to end.'

'I will have patience,' Mr O'Connor replied and he listened carefully to Neal's tale of woe before commenting, 'I've heard that story at least fifty times. I'll tell you what the problem is. Your spirit is too warlike for a quiet life. If you'll listen to me, I'll tell you how to ruffle the calm surface of your existence and live to some purpose. Get married! As well as having taught mathematics, philosophy and knowledge for twenty-five years, I'm well versed in the art of matrimony. I'll guarantee upon the source of all my misery and by the contents of my afflictions it's my solemn and melancholy opinion that if you take a wife you'll find after three months you will never again complain about having too quiet a life and nobody to fight.'

Neal immediately took up his cudgel and snarled, 'Do you mean to say that any woman could make me afraid? Say that again and I'll thrash you within an inch of your life.'

'I won't fight,' replied the schoolmaster meekly. 'I've been beaten too many times to feel I'd have a chance of winning. The spirit has long since been knocked out of me. I'm a mere selvedge, like one of your shreds. Haven't you seen how much I've shrunk over the last five years? Listen to me. If you want to taste the luxury of having a fight, if you are, as you say, blue-moulded for want of a beating and sick at heart because of a too-peaceful existence, get married. Neal, send my breeches home as soon as possible because they are needed. Good day to you.'

The tailor stood up, walked over to the door and looked out, with an expression of fierceness, reflection and contempt on the ruins of his once heroic face. The schoolmaster had suggested a plan of action and he decided to follow it with enthusiasm. He realised he'd been miserable because he'd sought the wrong thing. He remembered his relations were as ready for matrimony as they were for fighting so began to ask himself who he should marry.

Most men see a girl then fall in love with her. Not Neal! He fell in love with girls in general, then had all his feelings lined up and ready to apply to whosoever he chose.

The change in Neal's appearance was astounding. He expanded with this new spirit. The clothes he had taken in to fit his shrinking form had to be let out. He became gallant rather than martial. His eyes became more brilliant and less fiery. He came to the conclusion that he should spend all his energy in charming whatever fair damsel he selected as the object of his intentions. He decided he was in love.

'Neal,' said the schoolmaster, 'you're tempting fate. That could have sad consequences for you. You're not "in love"; you're suffering from universal passion, an entirely different thing. Resist it, I say, resist. I am, and have been for the last fifteen years, an advocate of staying single. The greatest luxury on earth is a single, solitary life. Think how happy the monks of old were. They grew fat and had double chins. Look at me. I was a solid man before I married. Now I'm wasted away. You know how many times you've had to take my clothes in since my marriage. Think, Neal, think. You don't want to risk becoming a nonentity like me.'

'Don't be daft! You can't think that any of the Malones should pass off this mortal coil without being either bate or married. If you help me find a wife, I'll promise to take your coat in next time for free!'

'Well then, what do you think of Biddy Neil, the butcher's daughter? You've always had a thirst for blood and I'm sure she can provide it! I'd say, if you must, marry her as fast as you can, though she's twice your size and three times as strong. Marry her, if you can. Large animals are placid and heaven protect bachelors from a small wife, who will rule the house with a rod of iron.'

'Say no more, Mr O'Connor,' replied the tailor. 'She's the very girl I'm in love with and I'll win her heart if it's the last thing I do. Now, come over to my house and we'll have a wee sup of the hard stuff to celebrate. Who's that calling for you?'

'Ah! Neal, I know that shrill voice well. You've heard the proverb, "Those who are bound must obey". I presume young Jack is yelling his head off and I must do something to soothe him. Neal, I suggest you think very carefully before you marry. In fact, I plead with you to reconsider and give matrimony a miss. Think before you take a leap in the dark. You could regret it.'

Neal had the heart of a true bred Irishman. He scorned caution as the mark of a coward. He abandoned all thoughts of fighting and, using all his courage, laid siege to Biddy Neil's heart. Like attracts like and Biddy, like Neal, was a fighter at heart. She could plant a body blow or a facer with great effect. Her prowess had only been witnessed by her immediate family, but there was no doubt in the opinion of her father, mother, brothers and sisters that given the opportunity to display her fighting skills to a wider audience she would distinguish herself! As a result, the tailor had no rivals in his courtship. He was completely alone in the field and there was no opposition from any of her friends. They appeared keen that the match should go ahead and shook Neal's hand with expressions more suitable for a funeral than a wedding.

The wedding passed off pleasantly. Mr O'Connor was invited but declined. He said he didn't have the courage to attend and had no wish to see any man's sorrows apart from his own. He met the wedding party by accident and was heard sighing as they passed, 'Ah poor Neal! He's like a cow going to the slaughter. I'm really sorry I suggested he marry. Soon he'll not be able to say he's "blue-moulded for want of a beating". That butcher will fell him like a Kerry ox and I'll have his blood on my hands. I should never have suggested that he marry. I'll feel his misery along with my own.'

About ten o'clock on the wedding day, Neal was rightly bluttered. His spirits were high and he was filled with love for humanity, so he danced with the bridesmaid. After the dance he sat beside her, chucked her under the chin and praised her appearance. Nobody seemed interested in Neal and the bridesmaid, with one exception. The new Mrs Malone stood up, then sat down again and knocked back a glass of poiteen. She got up a second time and remembered she was married to Neal. She was Mrs Malone! She must protect her man and keep him from sin. She rushed over to Neal, kicked him in the pants and knocked the bridesmaid down before picking Neal up, tucking him under her arm and carrying him upstairs to bed. Nothing was ever said about what happened in the bedroom; suffice to say, Neal came down the next morning looking very subdued.

Neal expected that once he was married his fighting spirit would return. About a week after his wedding there was a fair in the next market town. Neal brought out his collection of shillelaghs so he could choose the best one. He was determined to have a fight that day. His wife asked what he was doing and he replied, 'The truth of the matter is now I'm married I'm as blue-moulded for want of a fight as ever.'

'Don't go!' said his wife.

'I will go,' Neal insisted as he strutted round looking like a fighting cock. 'I will go! The whole of the parish will be unable to prevent me.'

In about half an hour, Neal was sitting quietly, getting on with his business instead of going to the fair. No one understands why he changed his mind.

At this point of his life, Neal was as fat as he had ever been, then he began to lose weight. After four months of marriage, he put on his waistcoat to go out and noticed how big it was. 'Well,' he sighed, 'isn't it wonderful how cloth stretches. This waistcoat certainly did fit me once!'

'Neal?' asked his wife. 'Neal, where are you going?'

Neal didn't reply. He swaggered across the room.

'Neal,' demanded his wife, 'this is the second time I've asked you. Where are you going?'

'Only to the dance at Jenny Connolly's. Don't worry. I'll be back early.'

'You're not going, Neal!'

'I'll go,' said Neal, 'even if the whole country should try to prevent me. Thunder and lightning, woman, who am I? I am Neal Malone, who never met any man who'd fight him! Neal Malone who was never beaten by any man. Why, tare-an-ounce, woman, I'll become enraged and play the devil. Who's scared, I say?'

'Don't go,' said his wife for the third time, giving Neal a threatening look.

'See you wee man, ye can't go!'

In about half an hour, Neal was sitting quietly, going about his business instead of going to the dance.

Soon after this, Neal and the schoolmaster met by accident. They stopped and looked solemnly at each other. Mr O'Connor was astonished by the amount of weight Neal had lost. The ghost of a blush crossed Neal's pale face. 'Why,' he asked, 'did the devil tempt me to marry a wife?'

'Neal,' asked the schoolmaster, 'tell me honestly: are you still blue-moulded for want of a beating?'

Neal didn't answer, but the next day he took his clothes in and continued to do so as his small frame shrank. His features became sharp with misery. He no longer carried a cudgel or looked as if he wanted to fight mankind. He looked downtrodden and walked as if every step brought him nearer the gallows. Before he'd been married three years he was so slight he had to put weights in his pockets to avoid being blown away by the wind. After a further two years, his friends couldn't distinguish him from his shadow, which was very inconvenient. At length he became suicidal and attempted to cut his wrists, but the stern Malone blood refused to flow out! 'I'll hang myself,' he thought, but again he was faced with disappointment. His body was so slight it refused to hang down on the rope he'd suspended from the rafters. It floated upwards, so he tried to drown himself, but his body was too light to sink. After that he shrank and shrivelled by slow degrees until he could not be seen, only heard. Gradually his voice became softer and softer, more and more indistinct, until it became impossible to say if the sound was just one's ears ringing. Eventually he melted away beyond mortal perception. As a hero he couldn't die. He merely melted like an icicle.

The schoolmaster's health has been restored. He's very happy. His wife died two years ago!

9

MATCHMAKERS, MARRIAGE AND MOUNTAINY FOLK

I am indebted to Frankie Bradley, who I met while having a cup of tea in a café in Gortin, who told me about his grandmother and how life has changed for mountainy folk. I am indebted to Evelyn Cardwell, who was education officer at the Ulster American Folk Park at the time, for telling me about the mountainy men of Tyrone and what they looked for in a wife, and to Francis Clarke, Patrick J. Haughey, Cormac McAleer and John Donaghy, with whom I spent what was for me a magical evening in An Creagán Centre in the Sperrins. Thanks are also due to the Marshall family and to Richard Knox for helping me trace them.

Mountainy folk lived in the Sperrins and other mountainous areas of Ireland. They never strayed far from home unless they were forced, by necessity, to seek temporary work in Scotland or England. Their supportive communities were isolated and considered travelling a few miles from home as a big adventure.

There wasn't any room for romance in the life of mountainy folk. Marriage was a practical necessity. It was very important to have a partner who would be useful on a farm. A big broad back that could pull a plough, draw turf like a donkey, carry two buckets of water and 'being so tall she could eat hay out of a loft, like a horse', were distinct assets for any woman in a mountainy man's eyes. If the woman either owned, or was likely to inherit, a piece of land, she was much sought after, even if she had the type of face he'd not like beside him when he woke up!

Regarding love and marriage, there were two types of mountainy man: the few who had the gift of the gab and sweet-talked a woman into saying 'Yes' and those with a practical approach. The sweet-talker underwent a shocking metamorphosis after marriage while those with a practical approach proposed marriage by saying something along the lines of, 'Would you like to be buried with my folks?'

There's a story about a mountainy man who sympathised with a neighbour about the death of his wife. The neighbour replied, 'Indeed an' sowl. She was a good catch and I've lost one good woman. She worked hard all her life an' we had a brave span together. The guts of sixty years!' Then he must have felt that sentiment threatened his reputation as a 'hard man' with a business contract rather than a romantic fool. He had to keep his manhood and independence intact so he added, 'Do you know what? I never really liked thon woman of mine!'

In the vocabulary of mountainy folk, the word 'love' was one to make fun of or to jibe at. They said, 'Love is an itchy feeling in your heart and you can't get in to scratch it.'

Frankie Bradbury said that when he became interested in women the only way of going anywhere was by your own effort, either by walking or cycling. Your horizons were therefore limited so you didn't have a lot of choice when looking for a wife.

Mountainty folk never made 'dates'. They went for 'a scud of a curt' or 'a set' and talked about 'your hoult'. If a boy appeared at the gate or entered the house of a girl, he was already half married!

After she was married, the greatest compliment that could be paid to a bride was that she 'was a powerful worker – in or out of the house'. The minute a bride entered her new home she had to show her paces in the fields. The prestige and reputation of her own family was at stake. All women were expected to be able to work hard and even hired girls were expected to work in the fields.

Another great compliment that could be paid to a mountainy woman was that 'she could make a meal's meat out of a dish cloth'. (The oral history of my family records that my great-grandmother,

Martha Henry, was 'able til make a meal out of nothin'', but then she
was reared in County Antrim!)

Before the Great Famine, three quarters of the Irish population's
diet consisted of potatoes and buttermilk. A working man would have
eaten a stone of potatoes each day, never mind the ones his wife and
children ate. The children took cold potatoes to school for lunch.
Potatoes and buttermilk constitute a balanced diet, with all the fibre,
protein, vitamins and mineral salts needed for health, with the exception of vitamin A, which is necessary for good sight. As a result, there
was a tendency for mountainy folk to lose their eyesight as they grew
older. If the farmer managed to grow carrots as well as potatoes, his
eyes stayed healthy because carrots are full of vitamin A.

Frankie Bradley said things became easier for mountainy folk after
the Second World War when the Labour government introduced the
National Health Service, free education and unemployment benefit.
His mother was able to boil a huge pot of potatoes over a crook and
crane. When they were cooked she drained the pot, threw a big cloth
down on top of the table and poured the potatoes on top of it. The
family sat around the table and helped themselves. His father 'heaped
a mountain of spuds on his plate, added a hunk of butter, broke an egg
on top and mixed the whole lot together'. Frankie said he didn't know
how his father managed to devour it! He said his mother was able to
make her large family a 'big fry' for breakfast using several inches of
animal fat in the pan and frying huge amounts of homemade soda
bread, bacon and eggs. Nobody worried about cholesterol in those
days and it probably didn't matter anyway because people were much
more active than they are today.

Young labourers were advised to 'never work for a woman because
she doesn't know what's in a day's work'. That was true. Mountainy
women squeezed two or three days' work into one. They had no
option because until about the beginning of the twentieth century
the menfolk couldn't earn a sufficiently large income from their
small farms to support their families. During the spring, the men,
helped by the women, did the ploughing or digging. Oats were sown
and the ground was prepared for growing potatoes. The men shaped
the potato ridges out of lea or grassland. Potatoes were commonly
grown using the labour-saving method of making 'lazy beds', so

called because only half of the land was dug and piled on top of the other half to form ridges. Manure was spread on the raised part of the bed. This was considered an economical use of a rare commodity. Manure was so precious that until knowledge of hygiene improved it was kept outside the farmhouse door to keep it from being stolen. The remains of lazy beds are still found on top of the highest mountains. They are proof that these inhospitable places were cultivated until the population either died or emigrated during the Great Famine.

Once the ground was prepared the men left and the Mountainy women did all of the remaining work. They spread manure the ground, planted potatoes, weeded and gave the crops the endless attention they needed. They attended the pigs, poultry and cattle, looked after their families and cared for the old folk – that is, if they were still around. The men didn't return until harvest time.

Prior to the Great Famine, when their children got married their parents gave them a share of their land. As a result, farms became so small it was impossible to live off them. After the Great Famine, this practice became illegal. Frankie belonged to a large family. There was no work locally so he was forced to go to England to look for a job. He said most of the Sperrin men went to the midlands, where they worked on roads and building sites. A lot of reconstruction was going on after the war and work was plentiful and well paid.

The right of a woman to make an independent income was generally recognised. She was in charge of hens and the dairy and she could keep her earnings. Profit from work in the fields belong to the farmer. The farmer's wife sold surplus eggs, killed fowl and dealt with a travelling buyer or took produce to market herself. If she was sufficiently wealthy to have a dairy she took great pride in it. Milk pans were placed on cool stone slabs, the floor was washed every day with clean water, the earthenware crocks, jars and wooden vessels were scrubbed, the churns, working troughs, paddles, rollers and butter-prints were kept spotlessly clean and proudly displayed. Mountainy folk would probably have had only one cow and a small dash churn, which would have catered to the family's butter needs, with a few pounds left over to sell.

The rural marriage rate was low. The mountainy woman was blamed because she could be bit of a tyrant, determined to bring up well-behaved, God-fearing children! Frankie said that until he got married, if his mother had caught him sneaking off to have a 'wee smoke' she fetched a blackthorn stick and blattered him with it! His mother was only 18 years of age when she married his father, who was 37! Young girls marrying older men was a common practice. Women tended to die young, worn out by hard work and childbirth, so men frequently had several wives, one after the other.

At the beginning of the twentieth century, the Land Acts came in. These caused mountainy woman to become seized with an urge to consolidate. Before that, tenants didn't own their land so people married young and it didn't matter much. Once a mountainy woman realised that she owned her farm, the marriage of a son, especially an eldest son, mattered in a material way. His marriage was felt to be a traitorous pulling-away of support. Comments were made such as, 'An' he goes an' marries, just as we were gettin' our heads above water an' risin' in the world'. A mountainy woman would give her daughters to somebody else's mother readily enough but God help anyone else's daughter who wanted to be her son's wife!

Mountainy children were expected to work hard around the farm. Work was mixed with play both before and after school. To say a son was 'a great worker' was to praise his ability as a manual worker. If a boy lifted his head in the fields, somebody would have guldered, 'Is it countin' the crows y'are?' Scholarship wasn't valued. It wasn't considered helpful when it came to earning a living.

The late poet Seamus Heaney was reared near Bellaghy. During the 1990s I met Hugh, who was one of his brothers, at the John Hewitt Summer School, when it was held in Garron Tower on the Antrim coast. He, like Seamus, had a lovely sense of humour and boasted he wrote much better poetry than his famous brother. When asked what he'd had published his response was a joking reflection of the views of mountainy folk in the past. He laughed and said, 'Do you think I've time for a lot of auld nonsense like thon? Sure I've a farm to run. The spuds need to be planted, the cows need to be milked, I have til plough the fields and dung out the byre. When would a hard-working fella, like me, have time to write poetry on paper? Sure, thon's no way to earn a living! I keep the farm going and my poetry's all in my head. It's much better than anything my lazy brother Seamus ever wrote!'

A Presbyterian minister, W.F. Marshall, summed up the attitude of the mountainy men of Tyrone very accurately in his verse 'Me an' Me Da'. It describes the difficulty faced by a young man who couldn't make up his mind about whether he should approach a girl he found attractive but who didn't possess a fortune and didn't have the type of body that would be considered useful on a farm or another girl, who was ugly but had land and who looked as if she would be a good worker on a farm. He dithered until it was too late. He remained a bachelor, who was lonely, miserable and uncomfortable as he grew old.

W.F. Marshall was born at Drumragh, County Tyrone, in 1888. He graduated with a Bachelor of Arts degree from Queen's College, Galway, before training as a Presbyterian minister in the Presbyterian College, Belfast. After that, he studied law before returning to work as a minister in County Tyrone. He was an academic who wrote in dialect. He had a keen sense of humour and a profound interest in his parishioners, who he observed carefully, enshrining their habits, speech and mindset in local folklore. His work is greatly loved by local people, especially those who live in County Tyrone:

Me an' Me Da

I'm livin' in Drumlister,
An I'm getting very oul'.
I have to wear an Indian bag
To save me from the coul'.
The deil a man in this townlan'
Was claner raised than me,
But I'm livin' in Drumlister
In clabber to the knee.

Me da lived up in Carmin,
An' kep' a sarvant boy;
His second wife was very sharp,
He birried her with joy:
Now she was thin, her name was Flynn,
She come from Cullentra,
An' if me shirt's a clatty shirt
The man to blame's me da.

Consarnin' weemin, sure it wos
A constant word of his,
'Keep away from them that's thin,
Their temper's aisy riz.'
Well, I knowed two I thought wud do,
But still I had me fears,
So I kiffled back an' forrit
Between the two, for years.

Wee Margit had no fortune
But two rosy cheeks wud plaze;
The farm of lan' was Bridget's,
But she tuk the pock disayse:
An' Margit she wos very wee,
An' Bridget she wos stout,
But her face wos like a gaol dure
With the bowlts pulled out.

I'll tell no lie on Margit,
She thought the whorl' of me;
I'll tell the truth, me heart wud lep
The sight of her to see,
But I was slow, ye surely know,
The raison of it now,
If I left her home from Carmin
Me da wud raise a row.

So I swithered back an' fort
Til Margit got a man;
A fella come from Mullaslin
An' left me just the wan.
I mind the day she went away,
I hid wan strucken hour,
An' cursed the wasp from Cullentra
That made me da so sour.

But cryin' cures no trouble,
To Bridget I went back,
An' faced her for it that night week
Beside her own turf-stack.
I axed her there, an' spoke her fair,
The handy wife she'd make me,
I talked about the lan' that joined
– Begob, she wudn't take me.

So I'm livin' in Drumlister,
An' I'm gettin' very oul',
I creep to Carmin wanst a month
To thy an' make me swol:
The deil a man in this townlan'
Wos claner raired than me,
An' I'm dying in Drumlister
In clabber to the knee.

W.F. Marshall

About twenty years ago, Liz Weir organised a storytelling festival in the Ulster Folk and Transport Museum. Ian Coulter, a much-loved storyteller from County Tyrone, got up and recited 'Me An' Me Da' by W.F. Marshall. Unfortunately, he suffered from every storyteller's worst nightmare – he not only forgot the words; he kept forgetting them! The audience were in hysterics laughing as most of them knew 'Me and Me Da' off by heart and kept prompting him. They transformed what could have been an embarrassing occasion into a star performance. I honestly thought he was, in local parlance, 'playing the goat'. He confessed afterwards he had done no such thing. His memory had genuinely gone blank. The audience's reaction reflects the esteem in which Marshall is held in Ulster.

Michael J. Murphy is another author who recorded Tyrone's folklore. He described how he was once in danger of being trapped by that well-known local character, the matchmaker. He had gone for a bicycle ride and arrived in the small town of Carrickmore on fair day. He saw the local matchmaker standing alone, watching the crowd haggling over the sale of a calf.

The matchmaker looked at Michael and spoke as if his thoughts were on anything but the possibility of making a match. 'Are you for home?' he asked. When Michael admitted that was where he intended to go the matchmaker said, 'Ride on and wait until I catch up with you.' He hurried into a pub. Michael did as he was asked, cycled several miles out of town, sat down on a stone wall and waited. He was joined shortly by the matchmaker, who said, 'I'm on a bit of a tedious mission.'

Michael immediately understood the 'tedious mission' was making matches between people who sometimes hardly knew of each other's existence.

The pair sat chatting for some time until they heard an approaching car. The matchmaker immediately jumped up to get a better look. He was clearly disappointed as it was overloaded with men whose faces were flushed from drinking at the fair. They drove slowly past and Michael realised the matchmaker was expecting somebody to arrive in a car. Eventually a car appeared and stopped. The matchmaker immediately got to his feet and pretended to be lighting his pipe as he carefully observed a woman and a girl get out. The matchmaker eyed the girl carefully then nodded approvingly. 'No lark's legs thonder,' he muttered. 'Yon one should be able til stand a bit of abuse.'

A basket and some parcels were taken out of the car, which drove off. The woman and the matchmaker walked along side by side, talking about the weather, the crops, the fair and everything that came to mind that was not connected with the job in hand. He watched the girl carefully. She kept her eyes focused firmly on the ground. Eventually the matchmaker asked, 'Is this a daughter of yours?'

'It is indeed.'

'She must be about 26?'

'Maybe you're right and maybe you're wrong!'

'Have you any more like her at home?'

'None.'

'Would you think of partin' with her, provided she's not spoken for, of course?'

The woman looked thoughtful before replying, 'I might if it suited her. She's quare and useful round the house.'

The matchmaker smiled, 'And what does the girl say?'

'Why don't you ask her? She's not stupid. She's got a tongue in her head.'

'I'd far rather you'd ask her yourself, ma'am.'

The woman bobbed her head, 'I'll neither put to or from her. You'll have as much bother asking as she will refusing.'

The matchmaker looked at the woman, 'You must understand, ma'am: I won't push this for myself.'

The woman replied, 'What odds? No one has tramped on anyone's luck yet.'

'Well,' said the matchmaker, 'there's no harm done. What I'm askin' is this, since it's gone so far. What ye want is a decent man, no one to call at his door for tuppence, sound of limb and mind, with no encumbrances.'

The girl looked at Michael. He felt the hairs on the back of his neck rise in alarm, so he jumped on his bike, waved goodbye and escaped by riding up the hill and away. In retrospect, he was very glad he'd done so because the matchmaker did make a match in the end!

In the past, mountainy men lived in isolated communities where the sense of community was strong. If a man needed an implement belonging to a neighbour, he was expected to take it without asking. Neighbours joined horses to form a ploughing team and they helped each other bring in the hay, harvest crops, including flax, and with 'spud hoking' (potato-gathering). Children, as well as women, helped the men in what was dirty, back-breaking work. Even today in rural areas schools attendance would fall during potato-harvesting time as the children would stay away to work in the fields. Schools therefore ensure their holidays fall on this period.

In many townlands, mountainy men did not like outsiders buying what they called 'a place' in 'their area', so they would often help one of their number to outbid a stranger.

The advent of television, cars, improved roads and public transport, the availability of cheap foreign holidays, better educational opportunities and so on have spelt the death knell of mountainy folk. They no longer exist, nor does the hard life they were forced to live. However, I was reminded of the closeness and honesty of mountainy communities when I asked Frankie if there was anywhere in Gortin I could buy petrol. He replied, 'There's a garage at the end of the village. You might get it a bit cheaper in one of the big towns, but they're decent folk in there and that's where we locals get our petrol.' I drove down the main street and pulled up at a pump at the garage. A woman came out and served me. I expressed surprise, saying I've had to pump my own petrol for years. She replied that her clients wouldn't tolerate that. Indeed, some don't even get out of the car to pay her but insist on giving her a bank card to use with her machine inside her shop! I left feeling very pleased that something of the old, caring, mountainy culture has survived.

10

THE RED HAND
OF ULSTER

I am grateful to Angela O'Connor of Ranfurly House Arts and Visitor Centre in Dungannon for information about the Hill of the O'Neills and the Flight of the Earls and I am also indebted to Dr Johnathan Bell, past Curator of Agriculture at the Ulster Folk and Transport Museum, for information about spades and ploughing.

I have a big confession to make. The more research I do about the Red Hand of Ulster, also known as the Hand of the O'Neill, the more confused I become. There are so many folkloristic versions of this story but they all have one fact in common: in the past, somebody, probably an O'Neill, was challenged to race across a stretch of water somewhere in, or around, Ulster. The individual whose hand touched the land first was promised the land as a prize.

Some of the stories say the race was to swim across the Irish Sea from Scotland to Ireland, which is possible, but highly unlikely. That particular swim is rarely attempted because of the coldness of the water and the danger of its currents. Many people have drowned attempting it.

Another story describes the race as being between two O'Neill brothers across Lough Neagh. The brother who was losing the race cut his hand off and threw it to the shore. That explains why the hand is red but it doesn't make sense. Lough Neagh is bounded by five of the six counties that comprise Northern Ireland. Surely if this were the real story, the hand would be called the Red Hand of Tyrone or

Antrim or Armagh or Derry/Londonderry or Down, depending on the direction in which the brothers were travelling?

The version I like best is the one about the leader of a fleet of Scandinavian sea rovers, who was raiding the northern Irish coast and felt that his oarsmen were not rowing fast enough. To motivate them, he promised to grant the land to the person whose hand touched it first. One man, called Niall or Neill, desperately wanted to own the land, but his boat was lagging behind so he cut his hand off and threw it. It was covered in blood when it landed on the shore and so he adopted the red hand as the crest of the O'Neills. It has become a familiar symbol in Ulster as it appears on some flags and banners, as part of murals painted on walls and on the badge of a baronet of the United Kingdom.

According to folklore, a left red hand is a symbol of the Catholic population while a right hand indicates Protestants. Catholic and Protestants in Ulster each describe those of a different religious persuasion by saying, 'S/he digs with the wrong foot'. That makes sense because Catholics in Ireland have a tendency to be left-handed while Protestants are more likely to be right-handed.

The soil in County Tyrone is very diverse. Farmers living there preferred to plant crops on their small farms with a spade rather than a plough. Spades were designed to suit all locations, types of soil and body types; 230 different types were once manufactured in County Tyrone! Some were designed for use with the left foot, others with the right. I once owned a turf cutter designed to be used with leverage from the left foot. It must have been a Catholic turf cutter!

11

BESSIE BELL
AND MARY GRAY

This story reflects the Plantation of Ulster's influence on County Tyrone.

A laird called Patrick Gray once owned a castle on the banks of Scotland's River Almond, which belonged to the estate of Lynedoch in the parish of Moneydie.

Patrick Gray had a beautiful daughter called Mary. She was the apple of his eye and he practically worshipped the ground on which she walked. He was also very fond of her best friend, Bessie Bell, the daughter of the Laird of Kinvaid. The fathers loved their daughters so much that they became extremely worried on hearing, during April 1645, that the deadly Black Death had reached Scotland. They knew the dreaded disease had decimated the population of Europe, as well as that of London. When the plague reached Perth in July 1645, they decided to protect their beautiful daughters by taking them to a secluded place a few miles from the Lynedoch Castle and leaving them there. They reasoned that if the girls didn't have contact with anyone they couldn't catch the plague. A hut was made from bushes, roofed with rushes and floored with heather. Enough food was supplied to last the girls for a considerable time. Unfortunately, the incidence of plague lingered on and on. The girls' food supply ran out, they began to starve and they were forced to forage to stay alive. They ate whatever they could find, including black snails.

Bessie had a lover who missed her terribly and was very worried about her. Eventually he discovered where she was, visited her and found the girls were on the brink of starvation, so he decided to go to them with food. He made several trips and the girls were very grateful. One day, when he was on his way to help the girls, he met a pedlar on the road, who had a beautiful, intricate handkerchief for sale. He knew Bessie would love it and bought it as a present for her. Unfortunately, the pedlar had stolen the handkerchief from the body of a plague victim that he'd found lying on the road. At the time the plague's grip was so severe that many people died wherever they happened to be and the countryside was littered with corpses. Bubonic plague is very infectious and the beautiful handkerchief carried germs within its folds. Bessie was the first to catch it. Mary nursed her as best she could until she too took ill. When Bessie's lover returned in a few days' time he found the girls dead, lying together with their arms around each other. Their relatives wanted to bury them in the local churchyard, but for some unknown reason that did not happen. They were carried to a ford over the Almond River and buried in twin mounds by the riverside. Years later, Lynedock estate was bought by a Major Berry, who erected a headstone with the girls' names on it and an unknown troubadour wrote the following song:

Young Bessie Bell and Mary Gray
They were twa bonnie lasses!
They biggit a bower on yon burnbrae,
An theekit it ower wi' rashes green,
They theekit ower wi' heather;
But the pest came from the burrows-town
And slew them baith thegither.

They thocht to lie in methven kirt
Amang their noble kin
But they maun lie in the Lynedich Brae
To beek forment the sun.

During the Plantation of Ulster, planters, who came from Scotland to County Tyrone, saw two beautiful rounded mountains side by side, which reminded them of the tragic story of Bessie Bell and Mary Gray, so they named them after the girls.

There's another version of this story said to have been written in the sixteenth century, but I don't like it nearly as much. It's about a lesbian couple who, on account of their sexuality, were shunned by the town's population and had to go and live in the woods. They paid a boy to bring them groceries and he accidentally infected them with the plague. The local church considered their behaviour sacrilegious and wouldn't allow them to be buried in the churchyard so their bones were tossed over the wall onto the heath.

Another version refers in a sly manner to Queen Mary I of England and her sister Queen Elizabeth I:

Bessy kept the gairden gate,
An' Mary kept the pantry;
Bessie Bell had aye tae wait,
While Mary peeved in plenty.

12

THE TAILOR AND
THE WITCH

Folklore is full of tales about witches who could shapeshift into humans or animals at will. Cows and hares are commonly thought of as animals that may be witches in disguise. Linda Ballard, who was working at the Ulster Folk and Transport Museum at the time, shared this story about the witch and the tailor. I love telling it to children because they usually cannot resist looking for a patch of fur in their hair!

In the past, children who had difficulty walking often became tailors because they could earn a livelihood by sitting sewing. They travelled around the countryside with a list of clients they visited regularly, doing whatever task they were asked to do. If a coat, skirt, blouse or suit became shabby, the tailor could recycle it by carefully unpicking the seams, turning the garment inside out and sewing it up again, so it looked like new, or he would make new clothes out of cloth supplied to him by his client.

Once upon a time, there was a tailor who unknowingly went to work for a witch. She lived alone in a small, single-roomed cottage. Each night she slept in an offshoot bed beside the fire while he was given a straw-filled mattress in the half-loft to sleep on. He had to sprockle up a ladder to get there. Once he was in position, he could peek over the edge of his sleeping quarters and see what was going on down in the room below.

One morning he woke up and sniffed the air. It felt strange, enchanted, somehow different from usual. There was no sign of any activity below. He guessed that the woman was still asleep so lay still and quiet, not wanting to disturb her. After a few minutes he heard the door being quietly opened. He peeped over the edge of the half loft and saw a huge hare come in, go over to a large barrel of water sitting in the centre of the floor and jump in. Within seconds the woman leapt out of it. The tailor couldn't believe his eyes. He spent the whole day thinking about what he'd seen. Surely he must have been dreaming?

The next morning, he woke up very early, looked over the edge of the half loft and watched quietly. He didn't have long to wait before the woman got out of bed, pulled the large barrel out into the middle of the room, filled it with water, walked three times round it, singing a strange eerie incantation, and jumped in. A large hare jumped out of the other side and disappeared through the door. The tailor thought it would be prudent to pretend to be asleep so he turned over onto his back and waited. Sure enough, the hare returned after about an hour, jumped into the water and out came the woman. The tailor could hardly sew that day because his mind was in such turmoil. Had he dreamt the same dream for two mornings in a row? Could the woman really turn into a hare? Was she a witch? There was something strange about her. Could she cast a spell on him? If she really did turn into a hare, where did she go in the mornings? Could he find out? What would happen if he jumped into the water? Would he turn into a hare? Could he follow her?

The tailor woke up very early next morning, determined to find out what was going on. He watched as the woman prepared the barrel of water, walked three times round it singing her strange, eerie incantation before jumping in and turning into a hare. He felt very excited as he stumbled down from the loft, jumped into the water, leapt out in the form of a hare and rushed out the door. He was just in time to see her disappear through a gap in the hedge. He followed her into a field and up a hill, at the top of which there was a flat piece of ground. When he reached the top, he saw that hundreds of hares were gathered there, so he joined them.

A large, white hare was standing in the middle of the assembly. The moment he arrived it stood upright on its back feet, sniffed the air and shouted, 'There's a stranger in our midst! Danger! We'd better scatter.' The hares immediately turned tail and ran away in all directions. The tailor followed the one he guessed to be the woman. She ran into the

'Scarper!'

cottage, jumped into the water, reappeared as the woman and he had just time to cover himself in water before she used her superhuman strength to empty the barrel. He returned to his normal self as the water flowed down the street outside her cottage.

The woman was raging. She howled fury at him. 'What have you done?' she shrieked. 'Why can't you mind your own business? I've a good mind to cast a spell on you.'

'Oh, please don't do that,' pleaded the tailor. 'I promise never to tell anyone what I saw. I'll be as silent as the grave. Tell you what, I'll gather my things and leave immediately. I've just about finished and you needn't pay me for the work I've done.'

The woman glared at the tailor as he gathered his things together and headed out the door. He was terrified by the look she gave him and apologised as he staggered out the door. 'Goodbye, m-m-ma'am. I'm very sorry to have offended you, m-m-ma'am. I promise I'll never utter a word about what I've seen.'

'One word of your experiences and you'll DIE!' screamed the woman.

The tailor was very relieved to reach the house of his next client. They were lovely people, who gave him a comfortable bed and fed him well. They had three delightful children who loved him and were always delighted to see him. Later that day, as he sat sewing, one of the children looked at him carefully. 'What's that you've got on the back of your neck?' she asked.

The tailor put his hand up to the back of his neck and shuddered with horror because he felt a small patch of fur behind his ear. If you are descended from the tailor, you'll have a small patch of fur somewhere in your hair, probably on the back of your neck. Do you?

13

THE CREAGÁN
WHITE HARE

I owe a big thank you to the staff of the An Creagán Centre (also spelt Creggan) for inviting locals to tell me stories that have been handed down through their families. Thanks are due to Francis Clarke, Patrick Haughey and Cormac McAleer for taking up the invitation. That was one wild night. I appreciate their stamina in fighting gale-force winds and pouring rain to come talk to me. The information they gave me was invaluable and we had great craic. *On the whole, it was a memorable experience that I treasure.*

An Creagán Centre is a local community venture established after the secondary school in Castlederg was closed and local children started attending secondary school in Omagh. They were very unhappy in their new environment because they were bullied and looked down upon by other pupils, who referred to them as 'them wans from the sticks'. Locals rightly thought, 'There's a lot to Creagán. We have the remains of a rich archaeological heritage, remnants of Celtic culture, a beautiful environ- ment and a very talented population. We should be proud of ourselves and teach our children to feel likewise.' A committee was formed and plans celebrating their heritage were drawn up and implemented. An Creagán Centre opened its doors to the public twenty-one years ago and has been a very successful venture.

Patrick Haughey told me the story behind the Creagán white hare. He said life was tough in the Sperrins during his grandfather's lifetime. I looked at the wild, windswept landscape, with its covering of purple heather and remembered the old saying, 'hunger under heather' – I thought that could be the understatement of the century! Patrick went on to say, 'Officially speaking, people ate nothing apart from potatoes and buttermilk but unofficially each family had a gun and somebody in the family who was a good shot! Poaching was considered fair game. People needed to live and landlords had plenty of money to buy food, so where was the harm? Hare, rabbit, salmon and birds were a welcome, tasty addition to local diets.'

In the past, white hares were common around Creagán. One of the farmers, who was called Pat Devlin, had a black dog called Black Nell, who was extremely good at catching them. She was so good that she became famous locally. People came from all arts and parts because they knew Black Nell would kill a hare for them. There was one hare, a big white one, that was so swift no dog could catch her, not even Black Nell. That hare was so fast and so good at evading capture that some people believed she was a witch. Others say that the white hare is a symbol of a rebel the authorities couldn't catch!

There is a stuffed white hare in the Creagán Centre and a large sculpture of it in a field on the road to Gortin, near the back entrance.

John Graham penned the verses describing the hare's antics. Patrick Haughey said the verses did not become famous until about fifty years after they were written and were set to music. It is now part of the local school's curriculum:

In the lowlands of Creagán there lived a white hare,
As swift as a swallow that flies through the air.
You may search through this world but find none to compare
With the pride of lower Creagán, our bonny white hare.

On a fine Sunday morning, as you may suppose,
When the bright autumn sun o'er the green hill arose,
Barney Conway came round, boys, and this did declare,
'This day I'll put an end to the Creagán White Hare.'

He searched through the mountains and he searched through the
    glens
And among the green bushes where the White Hare had dens,

'I'm a quare snick! Ye can't catch me!'

Till at last coming home on a lea rig that was bare
From behind a wild thistle out jumps the White Hare.

Bang went his gun, his dog he let to,
As swift as the wind the White Hare flew.
The dog soon came back, which made poor Barney sigh,
A sigh that the White Hare had bid him goodbye.

The next that came round, the truth I will tell,
Was a man called Pat Devlin with a dog called Black Nell.
He said, 'The White Hare, she will surely have fun,
It's twenty to one Black Nell will make her run.'

Now the hare she got up and his dog she slipped too,
And as swift as a swallow o'er the mountain she flew.

She made for yon meadows to cross over the burn
But, quick as the hare was, Black Nell made her turn.

Now on went the hunt, boys, it was lovely to see,
As the White Hare and black dog moved lightly and free.
Five turns the hare got by bonny Black Nell
And the ninth turn was given around John Haughey's well.

Now the hare made her way good as only hares can
Out into a lane that leads to Crockmacann.
It was there we lost sight of the hare and the dog,
But five minutes later after they came by the Black Bog.

So on went the hunt, boys, it was lovely and grand;
No doubt the White Hare is the pride of our land.
She came over by Esker where she knew the lanes well
And to the black greyhound the hare bid farewell.

There were some jolly sportsmen came here from Pomeroy,
Coalisland, Cookstown and likewise the Moy.
With their pedigree greyhounds they bought from afar
And they landed in Creagán in a fine motorcar.

Down to the lowlands the sportsmen did go
In search of the White Hare they tried high and low,
Till at last one brave sportsman on a turf bank quite bare
Cried out to his comrade, 'There lies the White Hare!'

Now they called up the dogs, boys, from off the green lea,
Where the sportsmen and beagles they jumped high with glee,
Right there on the turf bank they gathered around,
Nine men and seven dogs did the White Hare surround.

No wonder the White Hare did tremble with fear,
When she looked at the greyhounds, she raised her big ear,
She rose on her toes and with one mighty spring,
Jumped over the greyhounds and cleared through the ring.

On went the hunt, boys, like lightning she flew
Across the green meadows through bright morning dew,
But the pedigree greyhounds they did not go far
They came back and went home in their fine motorcar.

One day John McKenna was digging some ground
And was greatly surprised when the White Hare came round.
Said she to McKenna, 'Who's your man with the dog?
Don't you see him there yonder coming through the Black Bog?'

McKenna looked up, stuck his spade in the ground.
Says he, 'That's a poacher called Jimmy McKowan.'
'Ah well', says the hare, 'I can sleep snug and well
I thought it was Devlin with bonny Black Nell.'

Now to finish my song, boys, I think it is time;
I hope you forgive this little short rhyme.
If there's any among you has money to spare
Drink a jolly good health to the Creagán White Hare.

Hunting hares was a popular sport throughout the county. Geordie Barnett, who died in 1965, was a folklorist, local historian, archeologist, botanist and poet who recorded a story about how his father went hare hunting in 1862 with a party of local men in Cavanreagh. One of the men by the name of McKelvey was nicknamed 'Wee Willie'. He boasted that he had two very swift greyhounds, which had caught nine hares between them. James Smyth, another member of the hunting party, said he had a hare living in his grazing grass and he didn't believe any dog could ever catch it. Wee Will said he'd put his dogs to the test and the party set out for Smyth's grazing land. The dogs chased the hare all over the land. It tried every trick it knew to escape but it was eventually bogged down in mud and captured. It weighed 20 pounds and the dogs were completely exhausted after catching it. They recovered having once they were rubbed down with poiteen and given a good sup of it to drink! Unlike the Creagán White Hare, it was caught and doubtless ended up in the cooking pot because, as mountainy folk would say, 'You have to eat!'

14

FAIRY ENCOUNTERS

JOSEPH MCPHERSON AND THE FAIRIES

Thanks are due to Dr Mary Wack of Washington DC University, who gave me this story. She found it while in Ireland doing research for a book she was writing about diet in Ireland.

Joseph McPherson lived in the townland of Derryork, near Drumbane Fort. He was a farmer who, like many farmers in those far-off times, supplemented his income by working as a weaver. This was long before industrialisation, when weavers had looms in their house, so they could make linen after doing a hard day's work around their farms. Joseph McPherson became very upset because every night fairies who lived in the nearby fort came into his house and annoyed him by playing around his loom. They refused to go away and leave him alone.

One night, in 1804, the fairies invited Joseph to visit their fort and join them for dinner. He was frightened and didn't want to go but they were insistent and carried him off against his will.

Joseph was treated like royalty inside the fairy fort. He was given all sorts of delicious things to eat and drink before spending part of the night enjoying music and mirth. When the entertainment ended, the fairies took him out of their fort, away up high into the air. He was frightened and confused because he'd no idea where he was. He turned to the fairies and asked, 'Are you taking me up into heaven to the temple of God?' Fairies don't like being asked about God because they aren't sure if he is going to grant them eternal life or not. They were annoyed by Joseph's question and dropped him on top of a lime heap beside the fairy thorn on his farm. He was in a terrible state when he managed to stagger back into his house and told his wife and family all that had happened, but he had one consoling thought: perhaps he'd annoyed the fairies to such an extent by mentioning God that they'd leave him alone in future. That was not to be. Next evening, after he had finished his farm work and started weaving, he found himself surrounded by what seemed like thousands of fairies. The room was so crowded he could hardly move. He was in such a state of desperation he went and asked his clergyman to please come and get the fairies out of his house.

The clergyman found Joseph surrounded by fairies. He told Joseph there are two things which frighten fairies: the Bible and iron. He told Joseph to hold his Bible in his right hand and a penknife in his left and to accompany him reading a passage from the Bible aloud. To everyone's great astonishment, Joseph was suddenly whisked out of the door as he read. At first, he was bewildered because he didn't know what had happened. Then he remembered that iron may be used as protection against fairies, so he took his knife out of his pocket and formed circular patterns by passing it quickly around his body with the blade pointing outwards. After a few minutes he heard the fairies chattering and stood absolutely still, clutching his knife in one hand and his Bible in the other. He listened carefully and heard the fairies saying they couldn't possibly take him to dinner while he held a knife and the Bible. Joseph breathed a sigh of relief. He thought the fairies would go away for good, but it was not to be. They bothered him every night. They were such a nuisance that he eventually made a bargain with them: he promised to give them his firstborn child if they went away and left him alone. Shortly after that Joseph's wife had a baby boy. The child lived for two years before it was killed in an accident. Poor Joseph was stricken with grief and guilt. He blamed himself for his son's death because he'd promised his firstborn to the fairies. He became terribly depressed and thought he'd never find peace or be successful in Ireland. When he'd buried his son, he decided the best thing he could do was migrate to America. He sold all his possessions. He was sure the fairies would leave him alone and get on with their business around Drumbane Fort. It was not to be. Shortly after he arrived

'Yer man's away with the fairies!'

in America, he wrote home saying he'd enjoyed a pleasant peaceful voyage but the moment he arrived in America he found fairies from Drumbane Fort had crossed the Atlantic Ocean with him.

Lanty's New House

Lanty had no difficulty finding a wife. He had a tidy wee farm of about 6 acres, but he didn't have a house and it's a well-known fact that women are partial to men who own property. He found a suitable woman and told her he'd decided to build a house and settle down. She agreed to marry him. He walked all over his 6 acres and chose a site on which to build a house. It was one of those beautiful green circles said to be associated with the fairies. Everybody warned him against building there, but Lanty wouldn't listen. It was the most beautiful place on his farm. He owned the land and that was where his house would be, fairies or no fairies. He would not change his mind to oblige all the fairies in Europe.

In due course, a tidy wee house appeared on the site. Lanny got married, carried his new bride over the threshold and in the time-honoured custom of the Irish he hired a fiddler, got a lot of whiskey and invited all the neighbours in for a housewarming ceili. The craic was mighty, but while the fun and hilarity reigned a terrible groaning, straining and crushing noise was heard along the ribs and rafters of the roof. Everybody listened. It sounded as if thousands of little men were heaving and panting as they attempted to pull the roof down.

'Come on! Heave!' yelled a voice from outside. 'Come on, men. You know we must have this house down before midnight.'

Lanty was upset. He knew he couldn't fight the fairies. He went outside and looked all around. He couldn't see anybody, but fairies have magic powers. Lanty knew they were either hiding or had put on cloaks that made them invisible, so he shouted, 'Gentlemen, I humbly apologise for annoying you by building a house on a place belonging to you. If you will humour me by leaving my house alone this night, I promise to start removing it first thing in the morning. Furthermore, if you will tell me where you'd like my house to be built I'll put it there.'

A high-pitched voice replied, 'Well said, Lanty! Build your house between the two whitethorn trees above the boreen and we'll leave you alone.

'No sooner said than done.'

There was a soft sound like a thousand tiny hands clapping followed by a loud *SWOSH* as the fairies disappeared. Lanty never heard or saw a fairy after that, but when he started to dig the foundations of his new house he found a crock of gold. He'd obeyed the fairies so they made him richer than he'd ever dreamed.

15

THE PARISH PRIEST SAVES A PROTESTANT CHURCH

There was a wee Catholic man whose best friend was a Protestant. The pair went to school together, got up to mischief together, grew up together and started going to dances and courtin' at the same time. They were still best friends when they grew old and the inevitable happened. They were parted by death and the Protestant was the first to go.

It was the custom in those days to hold a wake lasting several days to show respect for the dear departed. A wake was a very sensible thing because medical science wasn't well developed at the time. People found it difficult to say if a person was really dead or had simply fallen into a coma. If the corpse sat up in the middle of the wake you knew not to bury it!

The wee Catholic man was very upset by the death of his friend. He went to the wake to pay his respects and spent the time eating and drinking poiteen. He was up very late the night before the funeral and, what with the alcohol and the emotional trauma of losing his friend, he slept in and was late for the funeral. He leapt out of bed and dressed as quickly as possible, putting on a black tie as a sign of mourning. He was late for the service and, as he'd never darkened the door of a Protestant church before in his life, he quietly sneaked into a pew at the back of the church and looked around. The minister was in the middle of a eulogy extolling the virtues of his dear dead friend. The wee man listened intently. The minister went on and on and on. The wee man was still feeling the after-effects of so much good poiteen. His eyes became heavier and heavier. He did his best to keep them open, didn't succeed and fell fast asleep. He was so sound asleep that he didn't wake up when he slid off the pew and onto the floor. He was very wee and very quiet, so nobody saw him or realised he was there. The funeral service ended, the mourners left church and the door was locked.

It was dark when the wee man awoke. He walked all round the inside of the church, looking for a way out. All the doors were firmly locked. He tried climbing up on the pews and shouting out the windows at passers-by, but nobody paid any attention because he couldn't be heard. Eventually he had a eureka moment! If he tolled the church bell, somebody was bound to hear and investigate. He climbed up into the belfry and began pulling on the rope. The bell sounded gently at first, then, as the wee man became more confident, it rang loudly. People in the village were alarmed. They thought the church was empty and a ghost was ringing the bell. A large crowd gathered outside the door. The Presbyterian minister was at a loss about what he would do until somebody suggested he send for the parish priest. Catholic clergymen are much more efficient that Protestant ones at dealing with spirits and ghosts and things that go bump in the night.

The priest arrived. It was very dark and nobody noticed he was carrying a rug over his arm. He looked at the crowd and said, 'I think there's an evil spirit inside the church. It should be dealt with before it does any harm. Open the door. I'll go inside and see what I can do.' He looked at the crowd and asked, 'Does anyone want to come inside the church with me?' Nobody did.

The priest lit a candle and held it aloft inside the church. He found the wee man, who was cold and hungry up in the bell tower, and asked, 'Would you like to play the sort of trick you and your friend got up when you were lads?'

'I wud an' sowl,' answered the wee man. 'It wud be a fitting tribute to someone who was a right ramscallion in his time.'

'Well,' said the priest, 'get down low so you're almost crawling. Keep low while I cover you with this rug. I'll get behind and chase you outside. I'll yell that I found the devil inside the church. That'll scare the crowd. They'll stand back and keep clear as I'm driving him out.'

'Yon was the quare geg!'

The wee man laughed and laughed. 'Thon's the quare geg.' He chortled. 'My dear auld friend wud love it. I'm just sorry he's not here to join in.' He bent down and the priest covered him with the blanket. 'Hauld on a minute,' he said. 'I'd better have a wee practice afore I go out and face my audience.' He ran up and down inside the church, pretending he was the devil. The priest could hardly keep his face straight as he watched his antics. Eventually he said, 'Come on! Stop acting the goat. You're ready to play your part and I haven't got all night. Break a leg! Run from the back of the church while I roar at you.'

The wee man went down to the stairs from the bell tower. The priest started yelling, 'Go on, ye devil! Get out!' He opened the door and chased the wee man into the street. The wee man rushed towards the crowd. Several people were so frightened they fainted and the rest ran home as fast as their legs would carry them. They thought it really was the devil instead of a Catholic man who was the worse for drink. From that day to this, they tell the story of how a Catholic priest saved a Protestant church.

16

LOUGH NEAGH

Thanks are due to my husband, George McBride, for giving me information about Lough Neagh, to Charlene Mullan and Pat Grimes for information and to my Granny Henry who told me the story about how the great Ulster giant Finn McCool 'lost the bap' with the giant who lived across the Irish Sea in Scotland and lifted a 'clod of earth out of Ireland to throw at his Scottish enemy', thus forming Lough Neagh and the Isle of Man. She used the old folk tale to subtly tell me losing one's temper is unwise!

I was raging. My wee sister had got up my nose big time. I must have had steam coming out of my ears I was in such a temper when I visited Wee Granny Henry. She asked me what was wrong. I told her my troubles. She said that by the time I went back home everybody would have forgotten about it and I should cheer up. She made me a cup of weak tea with lots of sugar in it, gave me a 'piece', consisting of fresh bread, butter and raspberry jam, with instructions 'not to tell mummy'. (I wasn't allowed to drink tea because mummy thought it was bad for children. Granny disagreed so she gave me tea, bread, butter and jam as a treat. It tasted like ambrosia!) When I'd finished my snack, she drew the sofa up to the fire and asked, 'Would you like to hear about the day the great giant Finn McCool lost his temper?' I said I would, so she put her arm around me, I snuggled up to her side and she began.

'Finn McCool was a huge giant, big and strong and scary. He used to stand on County Antrim's shore and glare across at a giant who lived in Scotland. The Scottish giant didn't like Finn and used

'I was so cross, steam was coming out of my ears.'

to shout insults at him. Finn was inclined to be stupid. Instead of either ignoring what the Scottish giant said or simply guldering, "Sticks and stones may hurt my bones but words will never hurt me", he decided to build a causeway across the Irish Sea, run over it in his seven-league boots and knock the melt out of the Scottish giant.

'One day the Scottish giant shouted such annoying things that Finn lost his temper. That's a bad thing to do because if you're in a temper you can't see things straight. If you feel you must do something, it's wise to wait until you calm down, then you're are less likely to do something you'll regret later. But Finn was in such a rage he didn't wait. He didn't even count up to ten, which is what you're supposed to do; although, in all honesty, if I'm in a rage I need to do more than count up to ten to calm down. I usually go and do something other than think about it, like go for a walk or get on with my housework. That helps. Anyway, Finn didn't do anything sensible like that. He bent down and picked a huge clod of earth out of Ireland's land and threw it at the Scottish giant. He was usually a good shot, but he was in such a rage he didn't take aim properly. He missed his target and the lump of earth he'd grabbed fell into the sea. It formed the Isle of Man and the hole left behind filled with water and became Lough Neagh.

'Now, just think,' said Granny, 'of the harm Finn McCool did when he was in a bad temper. He lifted whole families along with their homes and their animals and threw them through the air and killed them, so he did.'

'How did he do that?' I asked. 'Why didn't they just land on the Isle of Man and go on living?'

'Think about it. Some of the poor people would have been squeezed to death when he picked the land up in his huge hand, others would have fallen off and drowned in the sea, while those who managed to survive would have landed with such a thump they'd have been killed stone dead. It was a terrible tragedy, killing thousands of men, women and childer, and all because poor auld Finn lost his temper.'

Another story about Lough Neagh holds that a sixth-century earthquake threw up a large rock at Toome, which obstructed the flow of the River Bann, causing water to build up behind it.

Or you might prefer this tale about the origin of the lough. An old woman was the guardian of a magical well. She was trusted with the job of watching it and making sure it was kept covered and didn't overflow because the well's water had magical properties. If it started overflowing, it couldn't be stopped.

One day as she was tending to the well she heard one of her grandchildren crying. She rushed to see what was wrong, forgot to replace the lid and the water overflowed, drowning everybody living in the kingdom. That is why on a calm day if you are sailing on Lough Neagh and look down into its depths you may see the remains of a town under the water.

Another story is about the King of Munster's ambitious sons, Ecca and Reev, who decided they would like to have their own kingdoms. They travelled north, putting the seven ridges of Ireland between them and their father. Unfortunately, poor Reev didn't get any further than the great Plain of Arthven, where he was destroyed by a magical fountain. His name is perpetuated by Lough Ree.

Ecca was much luckier because Angus Oge lent him his magic horse from the stables of Brúg na Bóinne, which, as we all know, is where the sun god, Lugh, lives. The magic horse was large enough to carry Ecca and all his people, along with their goods and chattels, on the broad of its back, but it had one great disadvantage: it was lent on the understanding that it must not stop until it was returned to its owner in the stables of Brúg na Bóinne! When Ecca saw the Plain of the Grey Copse, he was so delighted by its beauty he forgot all about the bargain. The magic horse stopped, the whole rim of the Western world shuddered and shook and, as the hills of Ireland reeled and water bubbled up around their feet, Ecca jumped down and got his workmen to build a wall to keep the magic waters back! He asked his most trusted female friend to keep an eye on it. He realised that humans are frail and built a palace for himself beside the well so he could watch the watching woman. Over time a town grew up around the palace and the name of the Plain of the Grey Copse was changed to the Plain of Moneyreagh.

Everything went well for some time. The woman and Ecca grew old and grey and forgetful. The woman continued to watch the well and Ecca continued to watch her until one day a beautiful young lady appeared. She was gowned in the most magnificent dress, with silver and gold threads that shimmered in the sunlight. Ecca's attention was diverted. He was a normal man and normal men cannot keep their eyes off good-looking women. The 'watching' woman was filled with envy as she looked at the beautiful dress. She began to think of her youth and how beautiful she had once been. While she was dreaming, the waters burst out of the well and the whole town was drowned. You can still see the steeples and towers of Ecca's town shining beneath waters.

Lough Neagh has an ambiance of magic and mystery that defies definition. It is the largest inland waterway in the British Isles and one of the largest in Europe as it covers an area of 153 square miles. It is pre-glacial in origin and a treasure trove of the unusual; for example, Lough Neagh pollan is a type of fish not found anywhere else. (It probably gets its name from the Celtic word '*pollag*', meaning 'whiting'. Other closely related types of pollan are found in Lough Erne and the Shannon, but they are not the same as Lough Neagh pollan.)

Folklore tells of another endemic species of fish, now extinct, called the Lough Neagh char. According to local fishermen, 'they all went down to the sea and never came back'. Lough Neagh has a few deep holes where the char, which was an arctic species, lived. A more likely explanation is that they were overfished after the local fishermen discovered their hiding places. They became extinct around 1827. The Belfast natural historian John Templeton described them and made a drawing of one.

Eight rivers flow into Lough Neagh, but only one flows out.

The birds that breed around the lough's borders are strange, as are the plants. There is an interesting orchid called 'Lady's Tresses'. It is a North American plant not found anywhere else in Europe, except on the Scottish Island of Colonsay. There is also a rare northern grass called 'Holy Grass'.

Lough Neagh's western shore is bounded by County Tyrone. It's a dangerous place because the shore slopes gently into the water for several feet, then there is a sudden drop to a uniform depth of between 40 and 50 feet. At the north end of the lough, there's a narrow channel that's over 100 feet in depth. It was formed at the end of the ice age when the ice of the River Bann carved a channel to the sea. The currents in the lough are strange. Even in calm weather, they will suddenly appear, double up the pollan nets and drag the fishermen's floats under water. Another mystery is the peculiar booming noises that sound close one moment and miles distant the next. Sometimes these 'water canons' are associated with small whirlwinds, but the surface of the lake is never disturbed.

The lough is a place of change, an enchanted place where things happen that have never been written down. Secret sounds come from the fringe of the fen and parts of the mainland where cattle browse. They were once island breeding places of wildlife. New islands have formed, with new species and new growth, in this strange land of mystery, legend and folklore.

According to folklore, the water of Lough Neagh has magical properties that turn wood into stone. 'Lough Neagh hones; put them in sticks and take out stones.' Modern science confirms that the silica in the lough's water really does turn wood into stone. Pieces of silica-impregnated wood have been used to sharpen knives for centuries. There's a story about a fisherman who waded into the lough and when he came out he discovered his feet had turned to stone so he never needed to wear socks ever again! I wonder if he sharpened his knives on his feet?

17

FLANN O'BRIEN

Thanks are due to Nick Kennedy of Strabane Historical Society for information about Brian O'Nolan, alias Flann O'Brien.

Flann O'Brien was born on 5 October 1911 at No. 6 Bowling Green, Strabane. His real name was Brian O'Nolan, but Flann O'Brien is probably the name by which he is best remembered, so I am going to refer to him by that name.

According to Strabane folklore, Flann O'Brien had a strange upbringing. He was one of twelve children. His father, Michael Victor O'Nolan, was an eccentric Irish nationalist who insisted his children spoke nothing apart from Gaelic because he didn't want them to be contaminated by British culture. Young Flann learnt to speak English by sneaking into the local newsagent shop and reading comics under the counter. He, like his siblings, was not allowed to go to school, a fact that caused them to be treated with great suspicion by other local children.

The O'Nolan family lived during an age in which radio was in its infancy and there was no television. The children amused themselves by using their imaginations. Flann had a manic imagination and great originality. He had a fine sense of the ridiculous and a mischievous sense of humour. In his novel *The Third Policeman*, he suggested that policemen could turn into their bicycles:

> ... people who spent most of their natural lives riding iron bicycles over the rocky roadsteads of this parish get their personalities mixed up with the personalities of their bicycle as a result of the interchanging of the atoms of each of them and you would be surprised at the number of people in these parts who are nearly half

people and half bicycles. When a man lets things go so far that he is more than half a bicycle, you will not see him so much because he spends a lot of his time leaning with one elbow on walls or standing propped by one foot at kerbstones.

Flann O'Brien's upbringing enabled him to ignore rules he didn't like, a talent that proved useful when he suffered restrictions as a result of his job.

His father had a good job in Customs and Excise, so the family were well off. They lived in three houses in Strabane: the one where Flann was born, one on the Derry Road and a house on Ballycolman Lane, in which a ghost appeared when his father was away on business (see p.35).

In 1923, Flann's father's job required the family to move to Dublin and Flann was allowed to go to school. At last he was able to talk to his teachers in English. However, he said the happiest times of his life were those spent in his home town, Strabane.

After Flann O'Brien was awarded his degree from University College Dublin, he got a job in the civil service. That was, in many ways, unfortunate because the Irish Civil Service didn't allow employees to write letters, articles or books. Flann had writing in his blood and an independent mind, so he didn't allow a few rules to get in his way! His early upbringing had taught him to think of some way to negate anything he didn't like and he set about hiding his identity by inventing a series of pseudonyms. Flann O'Brien was one and Myles na gCopaleen another. I personally love that

'I do not see why the principality of the pony should be subjected to that of a horse.'

name! The literal translation is 'Myles of the horses' but he insisted it should be translated as 'Myles of the ponies' because he 'did not see why the principality of the pony should be subjected to the imperialism of the horse'. He often wrote letters to the papers using one of his pseudonyms, then wrote another one to criticise himself under a different name! As a result, scholars have found it impossible to collect everything he ever wrote.

Unfortunately, Flann O'Brien developed a problem with alcohol. He loved McDaid's pub in Dublin, where he met, and became friends with, writers such as James Joyce, Patrick Kavanagh, Anthony Cronin and so on. He didn't always approve of his friends and was overheard saying, 'If I hear that name Joyce one more time I will surely froth at the gob.'

He developed throat cancer and died from a heart attack on 1 April 1966. It is ironic that somebody who was so good at playing the fool should die on April Fool's Day.

18

TYRONE'S CUSTOMS, BELIEFS AND CURES

Thanks are due to Billy Sloan, who was born in Tyrone, Celia Ferguson, neé Herdman, Margaret Jones, Sheryl Dillon, Charlene Mullan, Vernon Finlay, Pat Grimes and John Dinghy for information about old customs beliefs and strange cures found in County Tyrone and Dr Nevin Hamilton, who told be how willow was used to cure headaches. Thanks are also due to Rachel Barlow, age 11, for the illustration on page 114 and to Tom Moore for describing how he was cured of Bell's Palsy.

The superstitions, habits, customs and beliefs of Tyrone folk are fascinating. One of the most interesting was the practice of fortune telling by reading tea leaves left in a tea cup.

Billy Sloan, who used to live in the county, told me about his old Aunt Martha's fortune-telling talent and how astonished he still feels by the accuracy of her predictions.

In the past, there was no such thing as a teabag. Tea was made using tea leaves and inevitably some of them ended up in the bottom of the cup. The fortune teller asked her 'client' to drink tea, leave a little, swirl it around and empty it so tea leaves were deposited around the inside of the cup. The fortune teller took the cup, examined the tea leaves intently and used his or her expertise to interpret them and foretell the future. A tea leaf shaped like a letter would indicate the imminent arrival of a letter while leaves gathered together to form a ship meant that a voyage was in the offing and so on.

One evening, when Billy was in his teens, he visited Aunt Martha and agreed to let her read the tea leaves for him. She said he would change his job, have to wear a dark suit, carry a briefcase and sail across the sea. He would meet a girl with the initials J.M., go out with her for several years, then break up, meet another girl with the same initials, end up marrying her and they would have three children.

Shortly after having his fortune read, he saw a small advert in the *Belfast Telegraph* for a travelling salesman. He applied, got the job and had to wear a dark suit and carry a briefcase. He went across the sea to be trained in England and met his first girl with the initials J.M., Joyce Montgomery. The young couple went out together for several years, then broke up, as predicted. Some time after that happened, he was mooching around the house when his friends called and asked him to go to a dance. He said he wasn't dressed and couldn't be bothered. His mother suggested that it would do him good to get out and his friends said they'd wait until he got ready. There weren't any showers in those days so he had a quick bath and dressed. It was very late, about eleven o'clock, when he arrived. In those days, girls sat at one side of a dance hall, hoping to catch the eye of a boy and be asked to dance. The boys stayed, grouped together, at the other side of the hall, where they surveyed the talent and decided who they'd ask for a dance. Billy saw a girl wearing a miniskirt and sitting on a seat. He liked the look of her and asked her to dance. Her name was Joy Montgomery, his second J.M.! (Joy was not in any way related to Joyce.) The couple started going out and eventually married. They had two children, decided, 'That's it! Two's enough!', then ten years later they had a wee late one, thus fulfilling the last of Aunt Martha's predictions.

Reputable fortune tellers never charged for their services. They believed that if they did their talent would disappear.

There were many other customs apart from reading tea leaves. For instance, many people believed that you must not pay a bill on New Year's Day to prevent continually having to hand out money during the following year. Others believed that anything thrown out before midnight on New Year's Day would bring bad luck. That included ashes, tea leaves and rotting food. Another thing you should never do on New Year's Day is hang out washing.

A number of housewives still believe cleaning windows on a Monday causes bad luck, as does brushing the doorstep or clearing out the grate on a Sunday. You should never cut your fingernails on a Friday or a Sunday. You should always tie your left shoe before the right one and never rock an empty cradle or stir your tea in an anti-clockwise direction – that's really asking for trouble because you're stirring against the direction in which the sun travels around the earth. It is very unlucky to leave a house by a different door from the one through which you entered and if you're given a cat you should butter its paws to make sure it won't wander.

During the spring, when the yellow celandines come into bloom (they look like buttercups except they have pointy petals and glossy leaves and are found on damp ground) put a bunch of them in the byre or in with your animals to keep them healthy and bring them into the house on 30 April to keep your family from becoming ill.

There are a lot of beliefs about the weather. For example, winter turns into spring because St Bridget warmed the rivers by dipping her feet into them. Folklore holds that St Patrick was jealous of St Bridget. When he heard she'd brought spring by dipping her feet in river water, he turned the stone and brought summer! Rain on St Patrick's Day will be followed by a wet summer.

If frogs lay their spawn at the edge of the pond, it will be a wet summer, while spawn laid in the middle of the pond foretells a dry summer. The behaviour of rooks in spring was used to forecast weather. If they nest high in trees, it will be a good summer and if the nests are low the summer will be bad. If cows lie down in the field, it's going to rain. Another saying, which is most likely true in Tyrone, is, 'If you can see the hills it's going to rain. If you can't see them, it's raining!'

There is an old saying, 'Never cast a clout 'til May be out'. (In the past, poverty-stricken people sewed themselves into red flannel at the beginning of winter and removed it when the weather became warmer. The old saying has two possible meanings: 'May' could either refer to the month of May or to hawthorn flowers.) People liked to get married in June because they had taken off their winter clouts and bathed, so they weren't as odoriferous as usual!

Many of the old customs regarding May Day still exist, such as the belief that it is the day the fairies move house so it's unlucky to throw ashes outside as they might accidentally hit a fairy in the face and that mishap would bring you very bad luck.

On May Day, you should never lend anyone anything. If you do, luck will be carried out of the house. If you have to give anyone a pail of milk on May Day, remember to add a pinch of salt to it to prevent luck being carried out of the house.

Pigs were thought to be lucky animals, so they were driven into houses on May Day.

It is very unlucky to see the *Cóiste Bodhar*, the Coach of Death. It carries a similar message to that of the banshee as it appears when somebody dies. It's driven by a dullahan (headless coachman) and pulled by either four or six black horses. Black horses are associated with evil and are ridden by villains while white horses carry heroes and princesses.

It is very unlucky to trip in a graveyard because you will almost certainly die that year!

You should never walk under a ladder. That strikes me as being good sense because the person up the ladder might accidentally drop something on your head!

Tyrone has a lot of folklore associated with fishing on Lough Neagh. For example, it is unlucky to drop a coin into the water while sailing in a boat because it will cause a storm to blow up. Before you go fishing, you should turn with the sun – that is, towards the south – for luck.

'Go away! I only carry good people.'

It's unlucky to meet a red-haired woman when setting out fishing because nothing will be caught that day. You might as well go straight home.

Friday the thirteenth is considered to be such an unlucky day that some Tyrone folk refuse to go out of the house. It is said that Jesus was crucified on Friday the thirteenth. The night before, thirteen had people sat down and enjoyed the Last Supper together. Out of the thirteen, one was captured and killed and another committed suicide.

The custom of bringing holly and ivy into the house at Christmas dates back to the ancient Celts. The druids believed evergreens possessed the secret of eternal life because they do not appear dead during wintertime. They thought the sun was in danger of disappearing as winter days became shorter. That was serious because without the sun's warmth everything on earth would die.

The ancient Celts held a huge festival, called Samhain, in midwinter in an attempt to end winter and bring the sun back. During this time, dwellings were decorated with evergreens.

St Patrick, like other clergy of the early Christian Church, adapted the pre-Christian festivals to Christianity and that's why we bring holly and ivy into dwellings at Christmas. It's also why we have wedding rings. A ring has no beginning and no end and so is regarded as a symbol of undying love.

There's an old saying about marrying:

Monday for health,
Tuesday for wealth,
Wednesday the best day of all.
Thursday for losses,
Friday for crosses,
Saturday no day at all.

If a robin flies into a house, a death may be expected in the family. It is thought to be unlucky to kill a robin because a robin tried to help Jesus when he was being crucified. It pulled a thorn out of the crown of thorns stuck into Our Lord's head. A drop of blood fell on its breast, turning it red.

Cows are another animal that figures frequently in folklore. The ancient Celts believed it was possible for a cow to turn into a woman and vice versa.

St Bridget was always accompanied by a white cow because she had a delicate stomach and that was the only kind of milk she could drink. If a snow white cow appears in a herd it will bring good luck. There are many tales about white cows suddenly appearing and providing the local population with unlimited amounts of milk.

I like the folklore associated with the human body. If your nose is itchy, you are going to have a fight with somebody. A hot right ear is as bad as an itchy nose because it also foretells a fight, as does spilling salt on the table. An itchy left ear means someone is saying something nice about you while an itchy right one means someone is saying something nasty, or spiteful, about you. If the palm of your right hand is itchy, you will meet somebody new while if the palm of your left hand is itchy, or sparks fly out of the fire, you will get money.

If you accidentally drop a knife, a woman is coming to the door; if you drop a fork, a man is coming. Another version of this holds that dropping a fork means somebody is coming. If you accidentally set an extra place at the table, you will have an unseen guest – that is, somebody from the spirit world, possibly an angel.

A tea leaf floating on top of your tea is a sign that a letter is coming.

If you wash your face in mountain dew during the month of May, you will be beautiful and healthy all year.

If one of your eyelashes falls out you should put it on your finger, make a wish and blow it off.

Crossing somebody on the stairs is very unlucky and if you want to bring somebody bad luck salute them with your left hand.

Breaking a mirror brings seven years' bad luck, as does opening an umbrella indoors and walking on the cracks in the pavement. Carrying a four-leafed clover brings good luck.

You should never put your shoes on the table because that's very unlucky.

It's also very unlucky for a pregnant woman to meet a hare because it will cause her baby to be born with a hare lip.

Menstruating women should never wash their hair because the water will cause blood to pass over their brains and kill them. Eating hair is another way to kill yourself because the hair becomes twisted inside your intestines.

Sneezes are dangerous and you should always say 'God bless you' or 'Bless you' when a person sneezes because the soul comes out of the body and there's a good chance that Satan will capture it, but if it is blessed he can't touch it.

The following rhyme is common in Tyrone:

Sneeze on Monday, sneeze for danger.
Sneeze on Tuesday, kiss a stranger.
Sneeze on Wednesday, get a letter.
Sneeze on Thursday, may be better.
Sneeze on a Friday, that's for sorrow.
Sneeze on Saturday, love comes tomorrow.
Sneeze not on Sunday, but pray.

COMMON CURES FOUND IN TYRONE

I am very grateful to John Dinghy for giving me a copy of Monica Haughey's fascinating book Out of the Embers, *published by the Creagán Community Centre. I gleaned a lot of the following information from it. Thanks are also due to Margaret Jones and Seryl Dillon for telling me about folk cures; to Tom Moore, who told me about how his Bell's palsy was cured; and to Dr Jonathan Bardon for information about sweat houses and to Patrick Sweeney in Pennsylvania, who told me about his experience in a Native American sweat tent. Native American culture is in some ways very similar to Celtic culture.*

Of the old folk cures listed below, I think some are nonsensical, some have a placebo effect and some may actually work!

Healers and Healing

Before the free National Health Service was introduced in 1948, the majority of the population could not afford the services of a doctor. Sometimes local councillors had doctors' fees reduced, or waived, if a family needed medical help and couldn't pay for it. This reduction was commonly referred as the 'Red Line' and it resulted in such poor payment it didn't act as a strong incentive for a doctor to spend time making his way over the mountainous terrain of Creagán. People had to be very sick before they sent for a doctor and admitting to needing one was looked upon as a sign of weakness.

Geordie Barnett summed up the general attitude in Tyrone by writing:

My name is Geordie Barnett and it's cruel is my fate,
For I had to call the doctors in, when feeling unwell of late,
For then and there they sentenced me, a fact which I deplore,
That I must bring my bed downstairs onto the kitchen floor.

Dislike of doctors was also common in wealthy families. Celia Ferguson (*née* Herdman), whose family owned Herdman Mills, told me, 'There was really no point in sending for a doctor because he could take three days to arrive!' As a result, people relied on old folk cures, an attitude that endures among some older folk today. They still prefer to be cured using folk medicine. I have heard several senior citizens saying, 'I don't like to go near a doctor. They give you medicine to cure whatever you've got, but sure it gives you something else! Better the devil you know!'

Some people in rural communities are recognised as having special healing powers. Some possess a multitude of cures while others have only one. The following people, who lived in the Creagán district, had cures. Johnny, known as Granny, had one for whooping cough, as did Mulgrew. All they had to do was breathe on the sufferer's throat to make it better. Joe Donaghy, known as Stephen, from Sultan, could cure a blockage in the throat caused by something being accidentally swallowed, as well as having cures for bleeding, sprains and blockages. He helped many people and animals during his lifetime.

I was told that the way people are named in the Sperrins is similar to how they are named in Donegal, with sons all being given the same name as the father. It meant that land passed from father to son without the bother, and expense, of changing names on deeds! (My father Paddy, who bought land from another Paddy McBride, reckoned that on paper it looked as if the original Paddy McBride was about 200 years of age!) The mortality rate among children was high, so giving all the sons the same name as their father acted as an insurance policy, but it could be very confusing. As a result, the child was given an official name and also one by which he was known, hence Paddy McBride, known as Fred. Of course, you wouldn't get away with that today!

John Conway had a cure for shingles, which involved the use of 18-carat gold, but nobody seems to know what he did with it!

Burns and scalds may be cured by the lick of a person who, at some time in the past, has licked a 'mankeeper' (lizard). Around Creagán, Peadar Joe Haughey was believed to have licked a lizard and to have that cure. John Connolly of Cretan was given the cure by the midwife at the time of his birth and Peter McGurk, from Sultan, also had it.

If a married couple have the same surname before and after marriage, they possess a cure for styes. All they have to do is take three briars from a gooseberry bush and use each one to touch the stye before throwing it over the right shoulder. Mickey McGuone had a cure for ringworm. He relieved the patient by drawing a ring around the infected area with a burnt stick or ink.

According to folklore, if you place an earthworm in the hand of a newborn seventh son and leave it there until it dies, the child will have a cure when he grows up. I couldn't discover what kind of cure that was but I am sure earthworms are greatly relieved to know families are much smaller than they were in the past, so the likelihood of dying in the hand of a newborn seventh son is extremely slim!

I had an old friend called Betty Quinn, who some time before her death fell against an electric fire and burnt her leg. It didn't heal and was very sore. She heard of a woman with a cure for burns who lived in Ballygawley. Betty was in a state of desperation so, although she didn't believe in 'that auld-fashioned nonsense', she decided to 'give it a go'. She got a friend to take her to Ballygawley and found the woman, who made her welcome and asked her in for a 'wee cup of tea'. While she was drinking the tea, the healer kept 'looking and looking' at her. Eventually she said, 'I think I can do something for you.' Betty said the woman came over to her and muttered something several times. Betty couldn't make out what she was saying, but her leg was better in a couple of days. She showed it to me and the difference was amazing. On the other hand, cures don't always work. Forty years ago, my husband had shingles. He was told about a woman in Aghalee with the cure. She gave him a belt to wear. It was made of white flannel, with herbs folded inside. It smelt peculiar, made his skin itch and didn't cure his shingles.

People who possess a cure do not charge for their services. Folk tradition holds that possession of a cure is a gift that must be freely shared. If a charge is made, the ability to cure disappears. Perhaps that's what happened to the woman in Aghalee? Her ability might have disappeared because my husband was charged for her services. It's acceptable to bring a gift to the healer, but money must not change hands.

Tom Moore developed Bell's palsy, which is a type of facial paralysis. The side of his mouth drooped and he described himself as 'funny-looking'. He was given medication by a doctor and it didn't work. Tom is a teacher and no teacher wants to face children while feeling under the weather and being 'funny-looking'. He was in a state of desperation when he heard of a farmer with a cure and decided he'd nothing to lose by paying him a visit. The farmer was working in his fields when Tom arrived at his cottage. His wife made him very welcome and sat him down by the fire while she fetched her husband. Tom said the farmer was a really nice man who took his ability to cure Bell's palsy very seriously. He said he'd inherited the gift from his father and had no doubt he could effect a cure.

Tom said, 'The farmer stood beside me and stroked my face. To tell you the truth I didn't like it. It felt peculiar to have a strange man stroking me, although I was aware that he was an extremely nice person. I think I might have liked it better if it had been a woman, especially if she'd been "a looker". I was told I'd have to come back two more times and after that I'd be cured. I offered payment, but he refused. He said the cure he had inherited was a gift and it was his responsibility to use that gift properly and pass it on. If he was paid the gift would disappear. I thought the whole thing was a lot of nonsense but I'd give the treatment a proper chance and not walk away early. To my great astonishment, when I was driving home after my third visit my face began to tingle. Then I found I could move my mouth. By the time I got home I was back to normal, completely cured.

'When I think about it, possessing a cure must be a terrible nuisance! Imagine, people expect to be able to turn up at your door whenever they want and you have a sacred responsibility to make them better. You've got to stop your own work and deal with them. It must keep you back and you can't even be paid for your time.'

People who possess cures are generally gentle modest people who take their gift, and the responsibility to pass the cure on to the next generation, seriously. They, like Tom's farmer, keep their method of healing secret. Of course, you might not be lucky enough to know anyone with a cure, so in that case you'd revert to one of the well-known old folk cures. The trouble with old cures is many of them have been passed on without actually saying how they were used! For example, 'willow is a cure for fever'. That is probably very sensible because willow was the seventeenth-century's aspirin, but what did people do with it? I wondered if the sufferer went and gnawed a willow tree or if part of the willow – probably the leaves – was boiled in water to make an infusion, which was strained, cooled and drunk. Then Dr Nevin Hamilton, who is a medical doctor with a great interest in local history, told me people cut a small piece of bark out of the tree and chewed it. That sounds more reasonable than chewing on a tree!

Cures for Arthritis
Get a cat to sit on your knee whenever you are in pain.

Eat three leaves of feverfew every day. (Medical science has shown feverfew to be of benefit.)

Put two horse chestnuts in the pockets of your trousers.

Mix a large thimbleful of gunpowder with a little milk, swallow and drink at least half a pint of milk before going to bed and covering yourself with warm blankets so you sweat a lot!

Wear an iron ring on the fourth finger.

Wear a copper bracelet.

Cure for Bed Wetting
Eat a fried field mouse (also called a grass mouse) on a butter cake!

Cures for Bleeding
Bleeding will stop if a cobweb is put over the wound. (This cure is sensible because the very fine fibres of a cobweb are sterile. They catch red blood cells, which helps the wound to clot.)

Pack a spider's web up the bleeding nostril.

The following rhyme, which is probably a translation from Irish, should be said. Was it said while using holy water? It seems likely.

Our Lord was born in Bethlehem,
Baptised in the River Jordan,
This water is good,
This water is pure,
In the name of Jesus stop the blood.

A nose bleed will be cured if a widow's key is placed at the back of the neck.

Roll up a piece of brown paper and place it between the teeth and upper lip. (Note: folklore holds that white paper won't work!)

Hold the points of a pair of scissors against the neck.

Rub your nose against a grave.

Cure for Bee Stings

Rub a blue-bag on the sting or cover with damp baking soda or honey. (Blue-bags and baking soda are alkaline and bee stings acidic, so this cure's sensible.)

Cure for Boils

Fill a small bottle with water, put it into in a saucepan of water and boil it for a few minutes. Pick the bottle out of the saucepan, using a pot holder, empty it and place the neck of the bottle over the boil. A vacuum will be created, which will suck the inflammation out of the boil.

Cures for Burns

Apply cow manure.

Rub butter over it. (My Granny Henry used that cure on me. It made the burn feel worse! All that happened was that the butter melted and made a mess on my dress! I'm glad she didn't try manure!)

Apply the insides of a goose.

Rub the burn with a raw potato.

Put slices of mushroom on the burn.

Dip a piece of brown paper in vinegar and apply it to the burn.

Rub the butt of a candle that has been used at a funeral against the burn.

Cures for Chilblains

Chilblains used to be very common. They were caused by toasting your feet in front of an open fire. Bad circulation caused the toes to swell and become very itchy. The advent of central heating has made chilblains less common. One of the old folk cures was to rub them with paraffin oil! I think that could be dangerous! Imagine sitting in front of an open fire with your feet covered in highly flammable paraffin oil!

Urinate in a biscuit tin and sit with your feet in the urine.

Cures for Colds

Celia Ferguson (*née* Herdman), who lives in Sion Mills, says her grandfather believed the breath of a dog was a certain cure for a very bad cold! Celia's uncle Rex Herdman wrote a very valuable book called *They All Made Me*. It records facts and anecdotes and bits of old family history that he had been told or gleaned from old letters. Unfortunately, Uncle Rex has not recorded how Grandfather Herdman took the breath of a dog. She doesn't know and neither do I!

Take a large clove of garlic, peel it, keep it in your mouth and bite on it every now and again so that its juices run round the inside of your mouth. You will be better in twenty-four to forty-eight hours. That might actually work, although I've never tried it. Garlic has anti-bacterial properties. Hanging a clove of garlic around your neck is said to keep the devil away. I wonder if chewing garlic has the same effect?

Eat a roasted onion before bedtime.

Put cow dung on your chest in the shape of a cross.

Burn an onion on a direct flame and breathe the fumes.

Eat some cinnamon.

Cut an onion into two, put one half beside your bed at night and leave the other half in your kitchen. Your cold will get better quickly because onion absorbs germs. When you get up, you must throw out the half onion left in the bedroom because it will be full of germs,

'They think my breath cures colds. Can ye credit it?'

but you may keep the one in the kitchen for slightly longer. (Folklore holds that when using onion don't keep and use leftovers – throw them out, because they destroy health.)

Cure for a Cold Sores
Rub a bit of ear-wax against a cold sore.

Cures for Deafness
If an ear goes deaf, anoint it with oil of eels.

Cure for Earache
To cure earache, roast an onion in turf ashes and place it against the ear.

Warm a little olive oil on a spoon and dribble it gently into the ear. (Make sure the olive oil isn't too hot! This was also said to cure deafness. This cure may work because a build-up of wax in the ear can cause both pain and deafness. The olive oil softens the wax so it may flow out of the ear. Olive oil may be prescribed today before wax is removed from ears.)

Put black wool in the sore ear.

Cure for Erysipelas

Erysipelas (large red blotches on the skin cause by bacterial infection, also known as 'the rose') may be cured by giving the sufferer a lump of butter. They must then take it outside and say a prayer over it while facing downwind, then apply half of the butter on the affected skin and eats the other half.

Cures for Sore Eyes

Drinking boiled daisies will take the red out of sore eyes. (My mother told me daisies are poisonous, so I'm not going to try that!)

A black eye may be cured by rubbing it with a tallow candle as soon as you can or holding a cold wet cloth against it.

Place a used teabag against the eye.

Hold a penny against the eye.

Cures for Fainting, Convulsions and Fits

It was said to be dangerous to get between a person having an epileptic fit and the fire because the fit could pass to you from the epileptic.

Epilepsy may be cured by heating a church key and passing it over the head of the sufferer.

Convulsions may be cured by throwing anything that can't be counted, such as salt, sand or clay, in the face of the person while saying, 'In the name of the Father, Son and Holy Ghost.'

The cure for fainting is somewhat similar to that for convulsions: throw grains of salt, sand or clay at the person.

Cures for Fever

First of all, warm your feet in hot water, then wash a pair of thin socks in cold water and put them on just before going to bed. Put a pair of dry socks over the wet ones. You should feel a lot better in the morning and your socks will be dry.

Use the juice of a willow tree.

Chop a raw onion and put the pieces in a linen cloth. Tie the cloth to the feet and by morning the fever will be gone.

Cure for Foot Cramps

Turn your shoes upside-down before going to bed.

Cures for Headaches

Place slices of raw onions on your forehead, then place a cloth that has been soaked in alcohol against the onions and tie it securely in place.

Grind some charcoal from the fire until it is really fine, mix with a teaspoon of water and swallow.

When you get your hair cut, take the clippings and bury them under a rock. If you do not do this a bird might use them to build a nest and you will suffer from headaches!

Rub the head with the corner of a sheet that has been used to wrap a corpse.

Cures for Heart Disease

Heart disease may be cured with the powdered root of lily of the valley or by using foxgloves. (Warning: foxgloves are extremely poisonous. They are full of digitalis, which is used by medical science to cure heart disease. Do not attempt to use this folk cure.)

Cures for Hiccups

Fill a glass with water, then put a spoon in the glass and drink the water with the spoon resting on your forehead.

Hold the bottom part of your ear while drinking water.

Hold your breath as long as possible.

'I'm fed up. The next person who wants to crawl under me'll get a good blouter up the hooter!'

Hold a penny between any two toes on one foot, then transfer it to two toes on the other foot.

Cure for Itch
Itchy skin may be cured by swallowing a small amount of bicarbonate of soda on a teaspoon before drinking a glass of water.

Cure for Jaundice
If a baby is born with jaundice, place it in bright sunlight. The sunlight will bleach the yellow colouration out of the baby's skin.

Cures for Sore Joints
Rheumatism may be cured by putting powdered washing soda in a muslin bag, which should be worn over the affected part.

Rub sore joints with poiteen.

Tie a large cabbage leaf around the joint.

Sweat houses are an intriguing way of curing sore joints. They were used by the ancient Celts and it is thought the early Irish wandering scholars introduced them to Europe. They are no longer used but several remain in County Tyrone, the one at Cadian being the best preserved. Cadian is 1 mile from Eglish and 5 miles from Dungannon.

Sweat houses were low, roughly circular structures, built from stones, with a hole in the roof and a small door. A turf fire was built on the floor and kept alight until the interior walls and roof became very hot. The fire was then poked out, the ashes scattered and the floor covered with rushes and the sweat house was ready for use. Naked people crawled inside, sat there and sweated. It was considered unlucky to sweat alone. Men and women entered together. When individuals felt they had had enough, they cooled down by jumping into any available water, such as a stream, river or pool.

Sweat houses are always found near fairy forts, so it is probably that they were used to facilitate healing, spiritual experiences by the addition of herbs and/or magic mushrooms to the fire. That aspect may have been brought to an end by the early Christian Church.

There is a great similarity between Celtic culture and that of the Native Americans. The ancient Celts believed, like Native Americans, that all life returns to earth, that one should take care of the environment and that great respect should be paid to trees, which should not be cut down without good reason. Patrick Sweeney told me about his experience in a Native American sweat tent. It seems similar to what probably happened in local sweat houses.

Sweeney is a member of the Quaker community, who are also known as the Society of Friends. The Friends' Church is very respectful of Native American customs. His church, near Yardley in Pennsylvania, allowed Native Americans to set up a sweat tent on their grounds. The Native Americans erected a tepee in the church grounds before spending several days burning a fire inside it until it was hot enough. (It must have taken several days for a turf fire to heat the walls of a sweat house to make them sufficiently hot to induce sweating.) Herbs were added to the fire.

When the Native Americans felt that the conditions were right, they invited members of the congregation to enter and spend the night in the tepee. Patrick, like the others, undressed, wrapped himself in a huge towel, ran out into the freezing Pennsylvanian night and entered the tepee. The atmosphere inside was stiflingly hot. At first he felt stupid and bored, sitting there sweating when he had better things to do. After an hour or so (it was difficult to judge time inside the tepee) strange things began to happen. Individuals began to cry and divulge things that had been troubling them. The atmosphere became charged. The distressed individuals were hugged and comforted in an extremely nice, loving fashion that was not in the least bit sexual. He wondered why people were confessing such intimate things until about six o'clock when he suddenly burst into tears and began saying how upset he was when his grandmother died. He was amazed because he thought he'd handled the death of his grandmother very well. When he came out of the tepee he felt as if a huge burden had been lifted from his shoulders. He realised his subconscious had been grieving the loss of his much-loved grandmother and he had gained tremendous relief from expressing his pain. The skin on his face had been covered in pimples that disappeared shortly after this experience.

Cure for Measles
Measles may be cured by giving the patient a mixture of nettle and garlic juice to drink. That's another cure that sounds sensible because

nettles are full of vitamin C, which bolsters immunity, and iron which makes the vitamin C more effective. Garlic has anti-bacterial properties.

Keep the patient in the dark for three days then give them a mixture of garlic and whiskey!

Carry a small potato in your pocket.

Cures for Pimples

Eat two apples first thing in the morning for six weeks.

Mix wheat flour with honey and vinegar and put it on the pimples before going to bed at night.

Protection against Winter Colds

Rub lard on your chest, cover it with brown paper and leave the paper on when you get dressed. (My grandfather said newspaper was just as effective as brown paper, but he came from County Antrim. He said that in the old days people had few clothes, so wrapping paper under their clothes was an effective way of keeping warm. It was great at keeping the wind out!)

Cure for Restless Legs

If your legs are restless at night and keep moving or suffering from cramps, put a cork under your pillow and a bar of unwrapped soap in the bedclothes at the foot of the bed. (I have never tried this but, unlikely as it seems, I know of an old woman who insists it works for her!)

Cures for Ringworm

Ringworm is a nasty, itchy skin complaint caused by a fungus on the skin of an infected cow. If the cow leans on a gate the fungus may be picked up by anyone who comes into contact with it. It is highly infectious. The fungus grows out from the point of contact and forms a ring. Applying a plaster containing a mixture of pig's lard, quicksilver, verdigris and Cross's Supplement to ringworm was said to cure it.

Ringworm will be cured if the healer applies saliva to it and makes the sign of the cross three times.

You can prevent your cows developing ringworm by tying holly to their horns.

Cure for Sore Stomachs

A hot cast-iron pot lid was wrapped in a cloth and held against the stomach to cure pain. The lid was reheated as often as necessary until the pain disappeared.

Take ginger.

Cure for Upset Stomachs

Dissolve half a teaspoon of baking soda into a cup of warm water and drink.

Tie a bunch of fresh mint around your wrist. (Peppermint has a soothing effect on the bowel. It calms bowel movements, thus easing pain. I think eating it could be more effective though?)

Cures for Sore Throats

To cure a sore throat, fill a sock with hot salt and wrap it round the throat. I was told that the stocking used to hold the salt had to be the one the sufferer had been wearing on their right leg that day. It was tied around the throat at night. Personally I think that could feel itchy and unpleasant, especially if the sock was smelly! What strikes me as more sensible is to eat local honey. I have found that soothing.

Cures for Styes

Styes used to be very common. They occur when the root of an eyelash becomes infected and swells, forming a painful 'bump' on the eyelid. It was said that styes can be cured by using ten gooseberry thorns, provided the sufferer's parents are still alive. Throw one thorn over the right shoulder before pricking the stye with each one of the other nine in turn.

Another method of curing styes was to point at a gooseberry bush while chanting, 'Away, away, away!'

Sewing needles were credited with magic powers, including being able to cure styes by touching them.

Bathe in cold tea from the teapot.

Run the tip of a black cat's tail over the stye.

Cures for Toothaches

Put cigarette ash into a tooth suffering toothache and say, 'As Peter sat upon the marble rock Jesus Christ was passing by. He said, "What ails you, Peter?" "I have a touch of toothache," he replied. Jesus said, "Rise up, Peter, and you will have no toothache and not only you but those who believe in this prayer."'

Toothache may be cured by chewing a clove of garlic or putting a piece of ginger in the tooth. (My grandmother gave me a clove to chew when I had a toothache. It did help.)

Rub whiskey on it.

I can't imagine how the next 'cure' could possibly work without killing the patient! Hammer a nail into the tooth until it bleeds then remove the nail and hammer it into a tree. The pain from the tooth will then be transferred to the tree! That's nearly as bad as the following 'cure': use your own teeth to pull a tooth from a skull.

Cures for Wasp Stings

Put a little vinegar on a cloth and hold against the sting.

Cover the sting in honey.

Cures for Warts

Water from St Colmcille's Well outside Carrickmore cures warts.

A wart will be cured if a funeral is approaching and the sufferer goes out, picks up a little clay, rubs it on the wart and throws it in front of the hearse while saying, 'In the name of the Father, the Son and the Holy Ghost.'

Rub a wart with a cut potato, throw the potato over the hedge and the wart will disappear as the potato decays.

(I do NOT recommend the following cure as it's cruel and I don't see how it could possibly work.) To cure a wart, stick a needle into a slug. The wart will disappear in the time it takes the slug to die.

(This is another cruel cure that is not recommended. Slugs have nerves and can feel pain.) Rub a black slug on a wart then hang it on a bush. As the slug dies the wart will disappear.

Rub a wart with a piece of meat and bury the meat.

Wrap mouldy bread and bacon round the wart.

Water from a smith's trough was thought to cure warts.

Rub nine knots of corn on a wart, then bury them or leave them somewhere they will decay quickly.

The juice of a dandelion will cause a wart to disappear. (I tried this cure on my daughter, Leona, who developed a wart when she was a child. The wart disappeared, but warts are caused by a virus; eventually the body becomes immune to it and the wart disappears. I have no idea if the old folk cure worked or if its disappearance was a coincidence.)

A daily application of the spittle of someone who is fasting will cure a wart.

The lick of a healthy dog will cure a sore on the skin. (I wonder if that would work? A dog's saliva is supposed to have antibacterial properties! Would it work on a virus? Dogs are said to cure their own wounds by licking them.)

I don't see how this cure could possibly work and it's cruel – hang a 'hairy molly' (a caterpillar) in an amulet round the sufferer's neck.

Spit on a wart every day before breakfast for two weeks and it will disappear.

Rub a piece of bacon on the wart then bury it in the garden.

Pick the wart so it bleeds, put a drop of the blood on a coin and throw it into the middle of a road. When the coin is picked up your wart will be transferred to the other person.

A wart will be cured if you're given a sliver coin.

If the above cures don't work remember the hand of a corpse was thought to be a cure for all diseases. Sick people were once brought to a house where a corpse was laid out so the dead hand could be laid on them!

19

Dixon from Dungannon

These comic verses are included out of respect and affection for their author, Crawford Howard, who was in his eighties when he died in June 2015. Before he died, Crawford gave me permission to 'do what I liked with his work'. I am very grateful to him and to his executor for allowing me to use 'Dixon of Dungannon'. Crawford has left a wonderful legacy of laughter. He never let his honours degree in languages interfere with his imagination, his sense of humour or his fine ear for the vernacular.

Now Dixon from Dungannon was a man of great renown.
Whenever things were going wrong around Dungannon town
Or yer oul' lawnmower was busted, or yer biro wouldn't write,
Dixon from Dungannon was the man to put it right.
The big air-show at Farnborough – a new jet was on show.
Prince Phillip and the Queen was there, but the jet just would not go,
An' this big lad wandered out and fixed her at a stroke
An' then he shouts up til the Queen, 'They forgot about the choke!'

Prince Phillip turns round all amazed to where the Queen was stan'in,
But she says, 'Don't be daft oul han'! That's Dixon from Dungannon.'
An' then she shouts, 'Hi! Dixon! Go home and get your Alice!
And bring her roun' about half nine for a pastie at the palace.'
The palace was in darkness when he brought oul Alice roun'
And the Queen says, 'Could ye fix that fuse, like, before we all sit down?'

So he fixed the fuse and they all sat down and began to smack their lips
As they ate the royal pastie and chewed the royal chips.

A volcano up in Iceland was causin' a lot of trouble,
So of course they sent for Dixon an' he got there at the double.
He says, 'Where's this volcano, for I'm the man til bate 'er.'
An' he got a lump of bubble gum an' stuffed it down the crater.
He then stood back and wiped his hands and says, 'Now calm yer fears!
I reckon that'll houl' her for about a thousand years!'
An' right enough it held her – now for miles around they come,
To watch her blowing bubbles outta Dixon's bubblegum.

'Dixon, come to the palace for pasty and chips.'

The Yankees was all very proud of their rocket til the moon.
When they found they couldn't get her back – that made them
change their tune!
So mission control in Houston, they sent word to Mr Nixon,
An' he says, 'There's just one thing to do! We'll send a wire to
Dixon!'
The reply came back from Dixon – 'Thon oul' rocket's just a wreck!
But adjust yer carburettor, lads, an' that'll get her back!'
So they fixed the carburettor and they muttered, 'That's her now!'
But Dixon from Dungannon was the man who showed them how!

Now poor soul Dixon died last week and up to Heaven he went.
St Peter says, 'You can't come in like – ye wouldn't be content.
There's never nothing wrong up here – there's nothin' needing
fixin'.'
With that the Devil wanders up, says he, 'Is your name Dixon?
For if it is come on with me, you know we'll treat you well,
There's a few wee jobs needs doing on the left-hand gate of hell.'
So Dixon says, 'Right! I'm yer man! And with the devil off he goes
And what the devil happened then the devil only knows,
But if things is goin' wrong in hell, ye can bet until this day,
That Dixon from Dungannon won't be very far away!

Crawford Howard

20

DEALINGS WITH THE DEVIL

THE LAWYER AND THE DEVIL

There once was a poor farmer who had three sons. He worried and worried about them. 'Sure,' he said to himself one day, when there was a north wind blowing and he was starving with cold while ploughing his field. 'Sure, this is no life at all, at all, at all. I'd give anything, even my very soul, to be able to educate my sons so they could escape into a better world.'

The words were no sooner out of his mouth than a tall stranger, dressed in black, appeared beside him. 'Do you really mean what you said?' he asked.

'Indeed in sowl, I do. I'd love to see my sons educated so they could enter a profession and escape from this terrible hard life.'

'Well,' said the stranger, 'I think I can help. Sell your soul to me and you'll become rich, but you must promise to come to me whenever I ask.'

The old farmer agreed, became very wealthy and was able to give his sons an excellent education. One became a priest, another a doctor and the third a lawyer.

Seven years later, the devil appeared when the father was alone, at night, with the priest. The devil said he'd come for the father's soul. The priest got down on his hands and knees and prayed and prayed for an extension of his father's life, which the devil granted.

All was well for seven years, when the devil appeared again and demanded the father's soul. This time the father was alone with the doctor. The doctor pleaded and pleaded for the devil to spare his father's life a second time and the devil agreed.

When the devil appeared for a third time, the father was with the lawyer. The lawyer looked at the devil and said, 'I realise you've been very generous and extended my father's life twice already. You can't be expected to spare him a third time, but do you see that candle sitting on the table? As a last request, will you spare him until that candle burns out?'

The devil looked at the candle burning on the table. It was only a butt and it would not take long to burn out, so he agreed.

The lawyer immediately went over to the candle, snuffed out the flame and his father's life was spared.

St Patrick's Purgatory

According to folklore, St Patrick once became very depressed. He was convinced he was a failure. He desperately wanted to teach the

'Thanks son, thon's dead on.'

Irish about the love of God, but nobody appeared to be listening. He was a sociable character, who found no difficulty in making friends. He enjoyed Irish culture and the *craic*, but the friendships he was making seemed superficial and lacking in depth to him. He longed to inspire people to give up their pagan beliefs and become Christians. He got down on his knees and prayed and prayed and prayed.

God answered St Patrick's prayers by guiding him to Station Island on Lough Derg. There he was shown a deep, dark cave and asked if he cared enough about converting the Irish to Christianity to come face to face with the devil and sample the horrors of hell. St Patrick said he did.

It's no longer possible to go into St Patrick's cave because the monastery, which had been built around the site, was destroyed on 25 October 1632, during the Dissolution of the Monasteries. According to descriptions of early pilgrims, the cave had a narrow entrance, with a door that was kept locked. There was a short descent of about six steps inside. The cave itself had two parts: the first being about nine feet long (three metres), followed by a bend and another, shorter space. It was not possible to stand up because the roof was so low, so one could only kneel. When the site was destroyed, the cave was covered by a mound with a bell tower on top of it.

Presumably St Patrick slid down the descent and crawled into the darkest corner of the cave, where he met and struggled with the devil. Hellfire made every bone of his body ache. He became faint with lack of food. His throat was parched and he was tortured by flames flashing before his eyes. When he came out of the cave he felt healed and cleansed of all sin. He had experienced Purgatory, which had prepared his soul to go to heaven after he died.

A monastery has existed on the site of St Patrick's Purgatory since the fifth century.

There are many islands on Lough Derg, two of which are closely associated with St Patrick. Station Island has the cave on it and was looked after by monks. They lived in beehive cells on the island. Those dwellings have since disintegrated and the only remaining trace of their existence is low circular walls. Today's pilgrims walk round them.

The other island associated with the saint is Saint's Island, on which a monastery has been built. Pilgrims come to Saint's Island in a spirit of penance and prayer. They are looked after by people working in the monastery.

In the past, pilgrims spent fifteen days fasting and praying to prepare themselves for the ordeal to come. Once they'd confessed their sins and received Communion, they underwent further rituals before being taken the short distance, in a *coite*, to Station Island, where they were locked in the cave for twenty-four hours. The next morning, the prior unlocked the door and, if the pilgrim was still alive, he was taken back to Saint's Island to undergo another fifteen days of fasting and praying.

St Patrick's Purgatory grew in popularity so that by the twelfth century it attracted visitors from near and far. It still does, although the rituals have changed dramatically. Pilgrims are allowed to wear shoes now, although the island's stones are still sharpened regularly to torture those who want to go the extra mile by walking in their bare feet.

'I'm knackered and
I've miles to go.'

21

TALES OF HUNGER

WANDERING SCHOLARS

Thank you, Gordon McCoy, for intriguing me with your knowledge of Irish, Ulster Scots and wandering scholars.

The ancient Irish had a love of learning. The art of writing was poorly developed and knowledge was passed on from one generation to the next by the oral tradition. Writing, as we know it, came to Ireland along with Christianity. This new skill was greeted with enthusiasm. Christian monasteries were established and became seats of learning. Monks copied books by hand. As a result, the Bible and collections of traditional Irish folk tales became available to scholars, who travelled throughout Europe, gaining and sharing knowledge. Many parts of these ancient paths travelled by scholars are present in County Tyrone. The reputation of the travelling scholars was such that Ireland became known as the Land of Saints and Scholars.

Rome was destroyed by the Visigoths during the fifth century. The Roman empire collapsed and what we know as the 'Dark Ages' settled on Europe. Ireland played a pivotal role in saving civilisation's classical and religious heritage.

Irish people have a reputation for being friendly and hospitable. Folklore records how eagerly Irish people, even those living in poverty, hosted travelling scholars. All they asked by way of payment was the opportunity to educate their children and soak up whatever knowledge was available.

There are stories found throughout Ireland, including in Tyrone, about a travelling scholar who arrived at an impoverished homestead. The farmer's wife boiled potatoes, took some out of the pot, then finished cooking the rest, which she gave to the stranger. He wondered about her actions and was very upset to learn the family, who had been so generous to him, were on the brink of starvation. They had fed him as generously as possible, retaining some half-cooked potatoes for themselves because they are difficult to digest. Hard potatoes remain in the stomach for a longer time than fully cooked ones, so hunger pangs are allayed for longer. There was also a strong belief that by offering hospitality to strangers you could be entertaining an angel unawares. That kind of attitude made the lives of travelling scholars comparatively easy in Ireland and explains how knowledge about Ireland travelled far from home.

A Sister's Love

I found this sad story in an old Fourth School Reader that I bought years ago for a few pence. I was surprised to find that it contained this reference to the death of two children who lived in Killeter village, near Castlederg.

Killeter is near Magherakeel Monastery, one of Ireland's most important ecclesiastical centres, situated along the ancient pilgrim trail through County Tyrone to Lough Derg. It dates from the sixth century but, unfortunately, only a small part of the wall of St Caireall's church remains.

St Patrick suffered toothache in the neighbourhood when he was returning from a period of Lenten sacrifice on an island in Lough Derg. He stopped at the ancient pagan holy well, now known locally as St Patrick's Well, or Tober Patrick, and is said to have drunk some of its water to relieve his pain. Folklore has not recorded whether the water worked or not, but it does record the story of a farmer who took his blind horse to drink at the well. The horse regained its sight but the farmer became blind. The well is said to have been so upset that it had cured a horse that it jumped to the other side of the road!

In 1848, Friday 1 December was a freezing day, with a howling gale and heavy sleet showers. It was not the kind of day on which you'd like to send a dog out. Ireland was overpopulated before the Great Famine and the majority of the population eked out an existence through sub-sistence farming. The McGath family, like hundreds of others, were hungry. The parents decided the best thing they could do was send two of their children to Castlederg market to sell a few eggs and use the money raised to buy a few provisions, such as oatmeal. Ten-year-old Ely McGrath and her wee brother set off. That year was during the toughest year of the Great Famine. By this time, poverty-stricken families like Ely's had sold everything they could to pay rent and buy food. As a result, the children were very badly dressed. Ely was wearing a thin dress and an inadequate shawl, with a woollen scarf tied around her throat. Her brother didn't have a coat or a scarf. He had just a thin pair of trousers and a well-worn jumper.

The shortest route from their home in Killeter was over Termon Mountain. The children finished their errand in Castlederg, had a short rest and set off up the mountain towards home. They had trav-elled the route across the rocks and heather many times and knew it well, although there wasn't a footpath to guide them. The weather was so awful that they couldn't see where they were going. Wind howled. Snow swirled. It became very dark and they got lost. There wasn't even a light from a friendly farmhouse to guide them. The poor wee souls became exhausted, gave up hope and lay down on the frozen ground. When they didn't return home, a search party was sent out to look for them. The children were found lying together, dead. Ely had wrapped her shawl around her brother's feet, her scarf was wound round his neck and head and she'd attempted to warm his hands by clasping them together, covering them with the folds of her dress and pressing them against her bosom.

22

SION MILLS: LINEN, CRICKET AND HYMNS

Thanks are due to Celia Ferguson and the Rev. Mark Greenstreet for information about Sion Mills and to the late William Reid's daughters, Pamela and Margaret, for permission to reproduce 'Calypso Collapse'.

I love Sion Mills. It is different from anywhere else I know. It has its own distinct, quirky personality. Even the name is different, an unusual combination: the Irish *'sion'*, which means the 'seat of Finn', or originally possibly *'sidheán'* (also spelt *'síodhán'* or *'sián'*), which means 'fairy mound', and the English word 'mill'. The village was established in 1835 by James, George and John Herdman, who con-verted an old flour mill on the River Mourne into a flax-spinning mill.

The Herdmans' family vision was to create a moral, God-fearing, educated, temperate, non-sectarian community. They built a model village with its own churches, school and recreational and sporting facilities. Their cricket team was the villagers' pride and joy. Their team was good and they knew they were good! They challenged the West Indies cricket team to a match in July 1969 and won! Ask any of the locals today about that match and they laugh before saying, 'Aye! But then we had Johnny Walker on our side.' In other words, they were very hospitable to the visiting team, who then couldn't hit the ball properly because they were 'eight sheets to the wind', a claim the West Indies deny.

The West Indies cricket team was on a short tour to England at the time. They had just played in a test match at Lord's, the result of which was a thrilling, high-scoring draw. They were full of confidence when they crossed the Irish Sea to play the provincial team of a small village. The match took place on the picturesque Sion Mills ground. There was a good crowd, the wicket was not bad, but it was damp with a good deal of grass. In twenty-five overs, the West Indies were bowled out for twenty-five! They said the wicket did not suit them because it was slow and they had just come from fast conditions. I know nothing about cricket but strongly suspect that's not a good excuse for an international team. I think the Johnny Walker tale is more likely to be correct! The score of twenty-five was the lowest ever against Ireland, the previous being twenty-nine, which was achieved by New York in New York in 1909. The previous lowest in Ireland was thirty-two scored by Scotland at College Park in 1911. The late William Reid was so delighted by the Sion Mills win that he wrote the following verses, which are reproduced by kind permission of his daughters:

The Calypso Collapse

On the second of July nineteen sixty-nine,
The excitement was keen, and the weather was fine,
In Tyrone's Model Village of fair Sion Mills,
Where the people awaited excitement and thrills.

For the West Indian cricket team soon would be found –
For the first time in history – on Sion's cricket ground.
When the time came to do battle with Ireland's team,
A sight of which villagers oft' times did dream.

No illusions were held what the outcome would be;
For hope for a victory never had we!
The question was only – how small or how great
The margins would be when our boys met their fate!

For a good fight at least was the best we could hope,
And wonder how long our stalwarts could cope!
But hope of a victory for Ireland's team
Was an outcome of which we had not dared dream.

The suspense it was great, the excitement intense,
As we watched the West Indies, their innings commence,
With one thought in mind as we glanced at the board,
Would a wicket go down ere a hundred was scored?

Oh! how little we hoped, or how little we thought,
That in two hours' time would such havoc be wrought!
And our bowlers and fielders create such a route,
To have all the West Indies for twenty-five out!

But O'Riodan and Goodwin – the men of the day –
Went through their defences like ploughshares through clay!
With the aid of such fielding n'er witnessed before,
The West Indies batting to ribbons they tore!

The throng of spectators sat stunned and amazed,
As if they on a modern miracle gazed.
And with loud acclamation their triumph did roar
When the Irish team crept past the West Indies score.

A victory for Ireland – we still can't believe,
The witness that day that our eyes did receive,
On that Sion Mills ground was a scene of a feat
That the players of Ireland may never repeat!

But from this day, no wonder each Irish heart thrills
Whenever they think of the name – 'Sion Mills!'
And the day the Calypso boys staggered and reeled
From the Irish attack in the Sion Holm Field.

Sion Mills has another claim to fame. It was here that the famous
hymn writer Cecil Alexander spent some of her girlhood years. She
lived in a Georgian house and it was while living there that she wrote
one of her most well-known hymns, 'All Things Bright and Beautiful'.
'The purple headed mountain' is a hill, called Meenashesk, to the
east of the village and 'the river running by' is the River Mourne, the
reason the Herdmans built the mill there.

'We bate them lads! We bate the
West Indian cricket team!'

When she was 27 years of age, Cecil cause a scandal in her family by marrying the Rev. William Alexander. He was six years younger than her! Her father was so upset he had the registers altered for the sake of propriety. In those days it was customary for a woman to marry an older man. That's why very old hymn books record her birth as 1823. The age difference obviously did not trouble either Cecil or William. They had a very happy marriage and produced four children. William became Bishop of Derry, where Cecil wrote, 'There is a Green Hill Far Away', when she was sitting with a very ill child. She looked out the window and saw a green hill outside the city walls that inspired her. Her husband was eventually awarded the Anglican Church's top position in Ireland, Archbishop of Armagh, but it was during her girlhood in Sion Mills that Cecil Alexander was first inspired to write hymns.

23

FOLK TALES ASSOCIATED WITH CHRISTMAS

WHY SPIDERS ARE LUCKY

The innkeeper's wife was very annoyed because she saw something she thought of as an ugly creature walking around on her nice clean floor. It was a great big spider! She lifted a broom and yelled, 'Get out, you ugly brute! Clear off! Never dare show your face inside my house again', and swept it out the door.

The poor spider was very upset. 'I'm so ugly,' he wept. 'I'm so ugly nobody could possibly like me. I'm so ashamed of the way I look I'd better go and hide. He found a tuft of grass and scuttled into it, but did not feel safe because people kept walking on it and he had to dodge their feet, so he climbed a tree. At first he was content. He had a lovely view and happily watched children playing below, then a sharp-eyed bird landed beside him. 'Oh!' thought the spider. 'If that bird sees me, it'll eat me.' He jumped to the ground and ran away in a panic. Eventually he reached a cave and went inside. It was very dark. He thought he was alone and began talking to himself. 'This is great. Nobody can see me, so nobody will be upset by my ugliness.' To his great surprise he heard another voice in the darkness. It asked, 'What makes you think you're ugly?'

'The innkeeper's wife! She hated the sight of me so much that she took a broom and swept me out of the house. I'm so ugly! I don't want to upset anyone else by being seen.'

'Beauty's in the eye of the beholder. Look around. We don't think you're ugly. Do we, folks? We think your looks are dead on, so we do.'

The spider's eyes adjusted to the dark and as he looked around he saw the cave was full of smiling animals. They made him very welcome. He climbed up into the cave's roof, became filled with ambition and began to weave a web. 'I'll make the most beautiful web in the whole wide world,' he thought. 'I may not be beautiful but that's no reason for not working hard to make something lovely.' He worked and worked and worked. By the end of a year, his web was beautiful, big and thick and luxurious. He was very proud of it.

One night, when he was fast asleep, he heard voices. He woke up and peered over the edge of his web and saw a newborn baby had been placed in a manger. The lady touched the back of the baby's neck, 'Joseph,' she said, 'the baby's cold. I don't know what to do. I've covered Him with everything I have.'

The spider thought his web would make a lovely cosy blanket, but he loved it. It was his pride and joy and he didn't want to part with it. Then he thought, 'I shouldn't be mean. That poor wee baby needs something to keep Him warm and I can always make another web.' With that, he cut the strands holding his web to the roof.

The web drifted gently down and landed on top of the manger. The lady looked up and smiled before tucking it cosily around the baby. 'Thank you very much,' she said. 'That was a wonderful thing you did. Would you like to jump down, come over here and look at the baby?' 'I would,' replied the spider, 'but I'm so ugly I'll scare you.' The lady laughed. 'I don't think you're ugly,' she said. 'Giving your precious web to my baby was a very beautiful thing to do. It was so beautiful I can grant you a wish.'

'Please! Please!' gasped the spider. 'Would you make me beautiful like a butterfly?'

'I'm sorry. I can't do that because beauty's in the eye of the beholder, but I'll tell you what I can do. I can make you lucky.'

From that day to this, spiders have been very lucky. It's unwise to kill one because that could bring you bad luck.

WHY ROSEMARY HAS A PLEASANT SCENT

God told the Holy Family to get out of Israel as fast as they could because King Herod intended to kill all baby boys under the age of 2. They packed their belongings and fled across the border to Egypt. When they first arrived there, they met a band of thieves who made them welcome. One of the thieves had a wife and a baby that was the same age as Jesus. There's very little water in the desert so it was practically impossible to get water to bath a baby. Somehow a thief's wife had collected enough water to bathe her baby. She turned to Mary and said, 'I don't see why this water shouldn't be used to wash both our babies. Tell you what, you wash your baby first. My baby has leprosy and I wouldn't want your wee one to catch it.'

Mary washed Jesus and his little clothes. She hung his clothes on a rosemary bush to dry. The bush received them gratefully. It was glad to be able to help the Holy Family and, from that day to this, Rosemary has had a pleasant scent.

When the thief's baby was placed in the water, his leprosy was miraculously cured. Folklore holds that the baby grew up to be one of the two thieves crucified along with Jesus, the one who said he deserved to be punished as he'd been a thief, the one who Jesus said he'd meet later in paradise.

WHY HOLLY HAS A RED BERRY

There was a terrible commotion in the hills above Galilee. The sky was cluttered with angels singing their heads off and shepherds chattering about a new star that had appeared in the sky. It was very bright compared to the other stars and it appeared to be moving. Eventually it stayed still and lit up the entrance to a dark cave on a hillside. The shepherds were puzzled. They knew that particular cave was used to house animals. They decided they'd better climb down the mountain and have a closer look.

One of the shepherds had a flock in which there was a newborn lamb. It was small and weak, so he picked it up and carried it as they moved towards the cave. When they reached their destination the star shone brightly right above them. The atmosphere became charged with wonder and filled with the sound of angels singing. The shepherds entered the cave and fell on their knees in awe. A beautiful young woman was smiling at a baby in a cradle. Her husband had his arm around her and three kings were on their knees, giving presents to the baby. The woman smiled. 'Come and see the baby,' she said.

The shepherds felt very awkward. They were just plain people dressed in working clothes, with muddy feet and dirty hands. What were they doing in the presence of richly dressed kings?

The woman must have read their thoughts because she said, 'Come on. Don't be shy. Remember that in God's eyes we are all equal, so don't let a few fliperti jipperties with rich clothes, jewels and crowns put you off. You have as much right to see the baby as anyone else. Stop standing at the door with your two arms the same length! Come on in. You're very welcome.'

The lamb was placed gently on the floor. He took his place beside the cradle, along with the shepherds and the kings. He stood up on his wee hind legs to get a better look. 'This is wonderful,' he thought. 'Wonderful!'

At last the shepherds began to wend their way back up the mountain. The little lamb trotted happily beside them. His heart was filled with thankfulness and awe at what he had seen. He didn't look where he was going and accidentally stepped on a small holly bush. Its thorns stuck into him. They hurt and he screamed. 'You hurt me. Why did you stick your nasty thorns into me?'

The little holly bush was upset. It was a gentle soul and didn't want to hurt anyone.

'I'm so sorry!' it exclaimed, 'I didn't mean to hurt you. I saw you coming, but I'm a plant. I'm rooted to the spot. I couldn't get out of your way. I really didn't mean to hurt you and I'm very, very sorry.'

An angel had seen what had happened and was touched by the holly's distress. She came and folded her wings around it. 'There! There!' she said. 'Don't you fret yourself. The little lamb isn't badly hurt. It wasn't your fault. He walked on you. He should look where he's going. Tell you what, you have shown such great compassion for the lamb that from now on you'll have a red berry.' From that day forth, holly has borne a red berry at Christmas to celebrate the birth of the Son of God.

24

THE FINTONA RAILWAY

I am grateful to the late Tom McDevitte (Barney McCool) for telling me about the Fintona Railway and making me laugh so hard I felt sore for days afterwards. Like Tom, I am really sorry it has closed. It would have made a marvellous tourist attraction. I am also grateful to the staff of Castlederg Library and to Christine Johnston of the Library of Emigration at the Ulster American Folk Park for being so helpful and providing a lot of information. Dr Nevin Hamilton, Florence Chambers and George Beattie were also helpful in this regard.

I have a confession to make. I'm not sure if the Fintona Railway should be called a railway or a tram. It was originally thought of as a railway, then, over time, it metamorphosed into a tram.

Perhaps in Ulster's Counties, today cannot be found
A place so void of changes as this cosy little town.
If Cromwell should revisit it, 'twould seem the same today
As when he placed his cannon on the top of Liskey Brae.

John Donnelly, 1926

Fintona's name is derived from the Irish '*Fionntamhnach*', meaning 'the fair watered land'. It's a very pretty, small rural town about 8 miles south of Omagh. In the 1830s, it consisted of one main street, which was about half a mile long, with a few side streets coming off it. It had five small water-powered mills, a brown (unbleached) linen market, a monthly fair for cattle and pigs and a weekly market on Fridays, which mainly sold oatmeal. In spite of its small size, Fintona had twenty-eight spirit shops! Apparently the spirits flowed over to such an extent that they resulted in frequent riots! The town was a social outlet for a wide area. A road, which was finished in 1829, passed through Fintona and linked it with Enniskillen and Omagh. It was decided to build a railway to Fintona in the 1830s because it would be very useful for transporting wood. The Londonderry and Enniskillen Railway opened a branch line to Fintona on 5 June 1853.

Once it was agreed that a link between Fintona and the main line would be useful, a committee was set up. It decided that railway lines should be laid along the track because hauling heavy loads along rails is much easier than transporting them along the rough paths acting as roads in the region at the time.

There was considerable debate over the type of power that should be used. It must be remembered that this was in the very early days of railway history, shortly after the invention of Stephenson's steam engine. Most of the committee members treated Stephenson's 'new-fangled steam engines' with suspicion. Even the dogs in the street knew they were unreliable, prone to breaking down and that they could explode. Eventually it was decided that the most reliable source of power was horse power. They bought a large Clydesdale horse and christened it 'Dick', thereby establishing a tradition. All the horses used on the Fintona Railway were called Dick. It didn't matter what kind of a horse it was – a mare, a gelding or a stallion – its name was Dick!

People were very class-conscious during the Victorian age. You were expected to know your place and stay in it! To do anything else was considered disgraceful behaviour. This class consciousness posed a big problem for those behind the Fintona Railway. How were the first- and second-class passengers going to be separated from the common working classes? The solution was simple: build carriages with an upper storey and charge a premium for sitting in comfort, sheltered from the weather, in the lower storey. As a result, the first railway carriages on the line looked more like a stage coach than a railway carriage! First- and second-class passengers sat inside designated carriages. Third-class passengers sat on the roof. It was very dangerous because of overcrowding. The driver was perched on the roof edge and could be pushed off and fall to his death. Horses can be unpredictable, so there were many other types of accident on the line and some of them were fatal.

The 'Dicks', who succeeded each other, were stabled overnight in a long shed. Little is known about the early Dicks but the last one was a gelding, looked after by the last driver, Willie McClean, who treated him like a member of his own family. Dick recognised Willie's footsteps every morning and used to whinny as they approached. Nobody could handle him like Willie. By the time Willie McClean was appointed in 1922, the design of the carriages had changed considerably. They now looked like a tram, not a stagecoach. Horse-drawn streetcars had been designed in America and were introduced in Belfast in 1872. Their design influenced the Fintona Railway so Willie had a coach that looked like city trams of the day, except that it had two compartments and could be pulled by one horse. Willie didn't have to perch perilously on the roof. He enjoyed working on the line until 1957, when it closed.

Eventually the strict classification by class was dropped and passengers could sit wherever they liked. There was one occasion when that caused difficulty. Most of the regular passengers had got on and chosen their seats when a crowd of gypsies arrived. Gypsies travelled around the countryside in caravans, so basic cleanliness, without a proper water supply, must have been impossible for them. They were odoriferous, to put it mildly. The regular passengers got off and complained to Willie, who dealt with it with his usual aplomb. He announced, with a perfectly straight face, 'Will all passengers in the back end of the tram please come up to the front because the back end is not going.' Surprisingly enough, that worked! The gypsies made sure they were in the first carriage and the other passengers got into the second.

Around 1947, a young lad called Jack Griffin worked as a boy porter on the line. One morning, when he arrived for work, there was no sign of either Dick or Willie. Eventually he discovered Willie in a small shed with Dick, who was lying on the ground. The poor horse was obviously ill. 'Will you help me get Dick up?' asked Willie. Jack did and they managed to get Dick to walk very unsteadily down to his stable, where he lay down again. A horse has to be really ill to do that, so his behaviour was a very bad sign. Willie noticed Dick kept looking down at his side and he said, 'I think poor Dick's in pain. He could have indigestion.' He mixed about a pound of Epsom salt and got Jack to help give it to Dick. It did no good, so they sent for Ernie Johnston, the local vet, who mixed a foul, black concoction, which looked like tar, in a basin. It took the three of them to get it down Dick's throat. 'There,' said the vet, 'that'll fix him.'

Willie replied, 'On top of what I've given him.'

'What did you give him?' asked the vet. When Willie described what he and Jack had shoved down poor Dick's throat, the vet shook his head and remarked, 'Poor Dick'll never get over that! You might as well give up and close the door on him.'

'When the vet left, Willie said, 'Here, Jack, come give us a hand. I'll no' close no door on old Dick. We'll ring him.'

They got Dick up and took him into the yard, where the process of ringing began. (To ring a horse, it is walked round and round in a circle.) The poor animal was very reluctant to move so, while Willie ringed Dick, Jack encouraged him to keep going by hitting him on the rear with a whip. After some time, the horse's sides began to heave and his stomach began to rumble. 'Look out, Jack!' warned Willie. Dick let fly, producing enough to fill a wheelbarrow, and there was a stench that is recorded to have been smelt all the way from Fintona to Dromore! Dick seemed better immediately and ate a hearty meal. He was back at work the following day. Willie blamed the trouble on Dick having eaten hayseed.

According to Nevin Hamilton, Dick never moved quickly! It took him ten minutes to cover the length of the railway line and people could walk

'Come on Dick, get up! An engine's not supposed to sleep.'

it in eight! Sometimes passengers paid the penny fare, got fed up with the speed at which Dick was moving, got off and walked the rest of the way!

It is easy to laugh at the original builders of the Fintona Railway for not seeing the advantages of a steam engine over a those of a horse, but then the past has an insidious way of affecting the present.

Today the standard railroad gauge is 4 feet 8.5 inches. That is derived from the original specifications for imperial Roman war chariots. The Romans were organised, efficient people. They ensured that all their chariots were standardised by having the same wheel spacing. Roman war chariots were drawn by two horses working side by side so the initial ruts were the same width as two horses' backsides.

Imperial Rome built Europe's first long-distance roads, including those in England. When coaches replaced chariots, they had the same wheel spacing. A different one would have caused the wheels to break when travelling for long distances over the original ruts.

People who built tramways used the same jigs and tools they had originally used for building wagons, so they had the same original wheel spacing. That resulted in the same gauge being used for railway lines throughout the British Isles because the same workers built both types of vehicle (Ireland had another rail gauge as well as the standard one).

Wagons used in America were originally built by workers from the British Isles. They have the same wheel spacing for the same reasons and so does the USA railway system.

Space shuttles sitting on their launch pads have two large booster rockets, called SRBs, made by Thiokol at their factory in Utah. The SRBs are shipped, by train, from the factory to the launch site, where they are attached to the sides of the main fuel tank. The railway from the factory to the launch site has a tunnel through which the SRBs have to pass. The engineers would have liked to make the SRBs larger. They were inhibited by the size of the tunnel, which was built using the ancient Roman measurements. Thus, what is arguably the world's most advanced transport system is based on the width of two horses' backsides, as measured by the ancient Romans thousands of years ago! As a result, I feel it would be unfair to blame those behind the Fintona Railway for not seeing the advantages of a steam engine over horse power.

25

FLINN'S ROCK NEAR NEWTOWNSTEWART

Tyrone's mountains frequently experience sudden, heavy rainfall around the middle of August. Water cascades into the rivers, causing the Lammas Floods. Suddenly gentle rivers turn into roaring torrents that frequently burst their banks, flooding meadows and corn and potato fields. One of these floods endangered the life of Charley Flinn in August 1812.

Charley Flinn was a wheelwright who lived in Newtownstewart. He had a timber yard, which was close to the river. He had been felling trees and decided to make use of the torrent to float tree trunks downstream because he was working some distance from home. He was in the process of handling a very big tree when the water flow suddenly increased. The sky became black and threatening. When he looked towards the river's source, he realised that there was heavy rainfall up there. He was in danger. The river suddenly became a raging torrent. Charley Flinn was worried about losing his large, valuable tree trunk. He attempted to control it by jumping onto it. He had barely got his balance when the men who were holding it lost their grip. Charley and the tree floated off downstream.

Men, women and children began running in every direction. Panic spread throughout the town about the danger Charley Flinn was in. Somebody got a long rope and threw it over the side of the bridge so he could catch hold of the end that dangled in the water. The tree bounced from side to side against the river banks with Charley, who wasn't a swimmer, clinging fast to it. It looked as if he would be dashed to pieces against the rocks when he had a lucky break. The end of the tree trunk got stuck in a cleft in the Giant's Finger Stone. Charley was able to crawl along the tree and reach the comparative safety of the top of the rock.

By this time, the entire population of Newtownstewart was lined along the river's banks, screaming, praying or shouting words of encouragement. The flood increased until it was obvious Charley was going to be washed off the rock. He fell to his knees and prayed. The flood washed over the rock and Charley ended up in the river. The crowd gasped in horror but Charley was lucky. The rope on the bridge washed out to him and he was able to tie it round his body. Men on the bank started pulling him towards safety. The rope broke and Charley sank under the raging torrent. Two men jumped into the river and hauled him out. At first, he was thought to be dead, but he recovered and was able to walk home. The rock was renamed Flinn's Rock in honour of Charley Flinn's lucky escape. It reminded mountainy folk living around Newtownstewart to be very careful when working around the rivers during the Lammas season.

River workers removed Flinn's Rock in the 1970s because it was thought to have a detrimental effect on the water flow. That could be true, but it certainly saved Charley Flinn's life. Until then, if you had gone downriver from the village of Newtownstewart and looked upstream towards the centre of the river, you'd see the large cubical stone mass that formed Flinn's Rock in the middle of the rocky channel.

26

ARDBOE

Many thanks are due to Richard Knox for being so helpful and to Pat Grimes for making folklore collected by Henry Devlin in 1948 and by Francis Quinn and Henry Devlin available to me. Thanks to Charlene Mullan for providing other information.

An old monastic church was founded by St Colman in 590 at Ardboe on the shore of Lough Neagh. It was destroyed in 1166 and then rebuilt. A magic white cow that came out of Lough Neagh during its construction produced so much milk that men working on the church had plenty to drink, as well as cheese and butter to eat. The excess milk was used as building mortar and proved very hard to chip. When the building was finished, the cow went back into the lough again, swam out, looked back and mawed 'Ardboe'. That's how the place got its name. '*Ard*' means 'height' and '*bó*' means 'cow', so 'Ardboe' means 'the height of the cow'.

There were very few cows in Ireland at that time, only sheep. The Ardboe cow was such a great milker she was coveted and stolen. Luckily the scarcity of cows meant that her hoof prints were easily traced. Each time she put her hoof on a flat stone she left a print. Sometimes the stones had not only a tracing of her hoof, but also that of her calf and the end of a pointed staff, where a man had leaned on it. These stones were used to trace her along the shore to Blackwater in County Armagh and on to Benburb. She was found and returned to Ardboe. A very close eye was kept on her after that.

According to Francis Quinn, one of the most important headstones in the graveyard is called the 'Friars' Stone'. The surname of this friar was Lappin. He was banished after the monastery was destroyed in the seventeenth century and had a price on his head. He had to keep out of sight and lived in an old mud hut with people by the name of Doorish. The descendants of the friar were buried on the other side of the stone in 1712. Ordinary people were buried facing the rising sun while clergymen were buried facing the setting sun.

One of the strange things about the graveyard is that after death women reverted to their maiden name. One of the headstones is engraved with the names of Bernard Lappin, who died in 1712, and his wife, Grace Kelly, who died in 1727. Another says, 'Sacred to the memory of Peggy Devlin, spouse of Dominick O'Farrell, who departed this life on the sixteenth of August seventeen twenty'.

The churchyard had both Protestants and Catholics buried in it, but according to Francis Quinn, after the seventeenth or eighteenth century, crosses were no longer put on headstones because it indicated that the graves belonged to Catholics and put them at risk of destruction.

During the tenth century, a cross was erected in the church grounds. It is the oldest in Ulster and is elaborately carved with biblical scenes. It is said to have been built with the help of the magic white cow. Rainwater filling the holes at its foot was regarded as holy water. People emigrating from the district used chisels and hammers to break edges off the cross to bring them luck. The district council put railings round it to stop that happening. The ancient abbey is near the cross and that, according to Henry Devlin, is where babies who were either stillborn or who died shortly after birth were buried.

There is a mark on a stone that is said to have been left by St Patrick's knee when he knelt on it many centuries before the cross was erected.

There is – or rather, was – a wishing tree in the church grounds. People used to come for miles around to make a wish to cure a disease or to put a curse on somebody. Healing was said to happen if you stuck a pin into the tree and then walked round it from right to left. The illness was transferred from the person to the tree. If you wanted to curse somebody, you stuck a pin into the tree, then walked round it from left to right and removed the pin. It seems as if more people visited the tree looking for healing than a desire to curse somebody because the number of pins stuck into the tree, and left there, caused it to become poisoned and die!

The cow wasn't the only animal to come out of Lough Neagh. A horse used to come up out of the lough at the Gollomom banks, feed for an hour, disappear and come back a year later at the same time, in the same place.

There's a strange place on the lough, called White House Flat. Men working there used to lift more nets than they set. Once, they were working from their boats when a monster rose up beside them. It scared the living daylights out of them and they made for the shore as quickly as possible.

There is an interesting underground cave (a souterrain) nearby in which the fairies were said to have lived. There is a story about a local farmer who fell into arrears with his rent. That was serious. Landlords punished people who failed to pay their rent by evicting them and knocking their houses down. The local fairies liked the farmer and lent him money. He was an honest man so he saved up and paid the fairies what he owed them. They were absolutely delighted and from that time on he was wealthy and his meal bin was never empty.

There is a very dangerous hole at Croswiggy. If anyone went into it, they never came out! Once a man went in playing his bagpipes. People listening outside heard him playing a tune a tune they knew well:

> I doubt, I doubt, I never will get out
> The further in the deeper O!

He was never seen again.

A ghost ship used to appear on the lough. She passed close to people but nobody could be seen on board. She hasn't been seen since the 1800s.

27

FAIRY LORE

Thanks are due to local musician, storyteller, artist and author Declan Forde, who introduced me to the late, great Conn O'Neill, who told me about fairies. I am also grateful to Francis Clarke, Patrick Haughey, Cormac McAleer and John Donaghy for information.

One of the many intriguing things about County Tyrone is that it's still possible to talk to very old people who believe in fairies. They are convinced of their experiences and find it difficult to understand why nobody, including themselves, ever sees a fairy today. Some say the fairies left Ireland because they can't bear the atmospheric pollution caused by oil-fired central heating. Others say the fairies are still here but aren't seen because people don't walk the way they used to. They travel by cars that are going so fast they don't have sufficient time to spot fairies, who come out after dark and disappear at first light.

Approximately twenty years ago, Declan Forde introduced me to the late Conn O'Neill, who lived in Pomeroy. Conn was in his mid-eighties at the time. He was a great old man who insisted he was the 'real O'Neill, not yon imposter who lives in Antrim!' He said his family were deprived of their proper inheritance at the time of the Great Famine. He insisted he had seen, and talked to, fairies and told me a story about a very lonely man who lived in a neat wee house and longed for company. One day he went to draw water from his well and what should he see but a beautiful woman rising out of it. He knew she was a fairy because normal women don't suddenly appear out of wells! He fell head over heels in love and the pair sat on the wall around the well and talked and talked and talked. She said she'd been

watching him for some time and had grown to love him. He asked
for her hand in marriage. She had tears in her eyes as she said, 'I can't
marry you. I'd love to be your wife but your house contains a lot of
salt. You use it to flavour your food. You'd be unhappy if you had to
eat meals lacking the flavour salt gives them but salt hurts me. If I was
exposed to it, I'd be drawn back into the well.'

The man looked at her and made an instant decision. 'Darling,' he
said, 'I care more for you than food. You'd add flavour to my life and
what more would I want? If I get rid of all my salt and promise never
to bring any into the house, will you marry me?'

The fairy agreed. The man went home, gave all the salt he possessed
to a neighbour and washed the floor carefully every day for a week in
case any salt had spilt on it. After that, the fairy married him and they
were blissfully happy until one day a neighbour called with a gift of
salt. The fairy cried as invisible forces dragged her back into the well.
The poor man was heartbroken and lonely for the rest of his life.

Monica Haughey, in her excellent book, published by Creagán
Visitor Centre, recorded stories told by old people who lived in
the neighbourhood of Creagán. Mickey Donaghy (known as Par
Oine), who lived in Sultan, told a story about Mickey Daly, who
had a bicycle shop in Carrickmore and repaired all the bicycles in
the neighbourhood. One day a policeman came into the shop and
said, 'We've had a very peculiar night. We heard people were making
poiteen in the glens in Sultan. We went to investigate along with the
sergeant and heard buckets rattling on a hillside. The sergeant said,
"Thon's the place. Go round the bottom of the hill and I'll go the
other way and we'll catch them." Off we went, right round the hill.
We didn't find anything. Whatever it was fooled us all night. When
we went to one place we'd hear the noise in another until eventually
we got fed up and returned home. Someone was pulling our legs. It
must have been the fairies!'

Sam Haughey heard the fairies hammering and said to Monica,
'There's two old crab bushes fornenst the house. I was shooting
rabbits; they were half a crown each at the time. It was summertime
and I went over one evening to the field, taking the gun with me. I
was along this garden at the bottom of the street, waitin' on a rabbit to
come, you know.

'This hammering started at the bottom of the yard down in the ground. You'd think it was a factory, the hammerin' going on. I got kind of feared anyway. It was after sunset. So I put the gun under my oxter and shifted home. Paddy went over next day and he heard the same down in the ground; in three different places under the ground.'

'Gentle places' still exist. They may be patches of ground, mounds of stone, bushes or fairy trees and they must not be interfered with in any way because that would annoy the fairies and bring some sort of misfortune.

Sam Haughey described what happened to a farmer when he tried to use fairy ground to grow potatoes. 'There was a wee place in Tornoge Mountain. This wee man broke into a field in the middle of the mountain that he thought was a dry spot. There came a wee woman to him and told him not to touch that place. It was the fairies' home. He said, "Go to hell, what did you do for my father's farm?" So he went ahead anyway. He opened it, spread it out and planted spuds. He carried manure up the mountain and put it on this wee field for the spuds. Well, they grew all right. And he dug them one morning and put them on the boil. Well, he left them until twelve o'clock at night and they wouldn't boil. This is no daft talk. This is true. They were as hard when they were comin' off as when they went on.'

Brigid Donaghy, who also lived in Sultan, had many encounters with fairies during her lifetime. They included seeing a man who was using a graip to fill a cart with pig manure. He turned round and in a split second the horse and cart were about 200 yards away. She was convinced the fairies moved them. Personally I don't blame the fairies for moving the pig manure away from their vicinity because it stinks to high heaven!

Pete F. McDonald of Copney retold a story about an old man from Copney who was courtin' a Conway girl from Crancussa. In those days, walking was the only means of transport. It was a fine moonlit night and as he reached the end of the road, where it meets the boundary bridge, he heard small young people singing an air he'd never heard before. He stepped into the side of the road to let them pass before continuing on his way. After he'd gone about a hundred yards he heard more singing and another group of small young people appeared. The moon was shining and he could see them clearly. He met different groups until he came to Alice Keenan's house, after which he didn't see any more.

Mickey Donaghy recounted a story to Monica about an old lady he knew very well, who told of how before she was married the priest prayed after Mass that fairies would be banished from the neighbourhood. She saw the fairies leaving Sultan in a chain. They were carrying lamps and came down from Sultan crossroads, down the valley, right down to the bog, over to the boundary bridge and away. 'They were smokin' pipes and wearin' hats and coats in a train where there was nothin' only a rough track.'

That story's very similar to the one Patrick J. Haughey said had been passed down through his family about the time the French fairies left Creagán. He wasn't sure where the story had originated but thought it could have been with his grandfather or great-grandfather, who saw a band of fairies marching smartly out of the neighbourhood. They were dressed like French soldiers, who, he presumed, came over to fight in the Williamite War and had decided it was time to go home. They were dressed very smartly in foreign military uniforms, complete with epaulettes and shiny buttons. They had a band playing and were accompanied by women and children who carried all their goods. It was obvious they were leaving and weren't coming back.

28

Woodrow Wilson and County Tyrone

Many people from County Tyrone, especially Presbyterians, were dissatisfied with their harsh living conditions and the persecution they suffered because of their religious faith. Presbyterians had left Scotland for the same reasons and did not have the same connection to the land as the native Irish so they found it relatively easy to leave in order to seek a better life in America. They were comparatively wealthy, sturdy, stubborn people who took their tools, music, Bibles and language with them. They forced their way into the wilderness, adapting quickly to their new surroundings, learning and using the fighting methods of the Native Americans. In America, they are known as the 'Scots-Irish', while in Ireland they are referred to as 'Ulster Scots'. Their influence is seen in many places, including the American Declaration of Independence and bluegrass music. An amazing number of influential people, including Davy Crockett, three American presidents, a musician who wrote popular classics, including 'The Hokie Cokie', and the inventor of Irish coffee all came from County Tyrone!

Woodrow Wilson was the twenty-eighth President of the United States of America (1913–1921) and his ancestors came from Dergalt, 3 miles from Strabane, County Tyrone. He is considered to be one of the most outstanding presidents America has ever had. He had a brilliant academic career before being elected and is the only President to have been awarded a doctorate (a PhD in political science). His academic background enabled him to oversee legislation, including the women's right to vote, that changed the face of the country. He was awarded a Nobel Peace Prize in 1919 and guided America throughout the First World War.

President Woodrow Wilson was born in Virginia on 28 December 1956, the son of devoted Presbyterian parents. His father was one of the founders of the Presbyterian Church in America in 1861. His paternal grandparents emigrated from Tyrone to America in 1807 and he was very proud of his Scots-Irish ancestry. In an address to a New England society at their annual banquet in Brooklyn on 21 December 1896, he said:

> I am not of your blood. I am not a Virginian Cavalier. But I come from as good blood as yours – in some respects better, because the Scots-Irish, although they are as much in earnest as you are, have a little bit more gaiety and more elasticity than you have. We believe as sincerely as you do that we really made this country.

His enthusiasm for family history was such that he visited County Tyrone during the summer of 1899 to carry out family research.

I first visited President Wilson's ancestral homestead, which is near Strabane, in the 1960s. At that time, it was occupied by a bewildered, elderly brother and sister, who said they were amazed to find they were descended from the same stock as an American President. They weren't entirely pleased about it! I can't remember their exact words but the gist of the conversation was that they were very shocked to discover their connection with the President. It had disrupted their lifestyle. They had been plain, contented mountainy folk who worked hard for a living and got on well with their neighbours when, suddenly, the place was heaving with media folk, who arranged things to suit themselves. They supposed they were much more comfortable than they had been, but they had no peace. People kept coming and going and sometimes they just wished to be left alone, although they appreciated the fact that they were no longer responsible for the upkeep of their cottage and they had an income from acting as caretakers.

I apologised, saying I was sorry to be a disturbance. They said they didn't mean me as I was 'all right'. They invited me to sit down by the fire, give them 'some of my *craic*' and have a 'wee cup of tea in my hand'.

I asked if they had ever been to America. The idea appeared to fill them with horror as they said emphatically they liked where they lived and they didn't want to go anywhere else.

'Have you never been away from home?' I asked. The sister replied, 'I used to cycle up to "The Plum".' She meant Plumbridge, a picturesque village a few miles up the road. 'I haven't been as far as that for years. What's it like up at "The Plum" nowadays?' She laughed when I admitted I'd never been to 'The Plum'. By the way, Plumbridge hasn't got an Irish name because a man, called Devine, who built the bridge, never used a plumb-line; instead, he established a straight vertical line by spitting into the river and using the line of the spittle, hence Plumbridge!

The old couple are long dead. Their cottage is kept in good repair and is in the charge of the Ulster American Folk Park. It is possible to walk around it. It's not always open, but tourists can peer in the windows, admire the spectacular views and read the interesting notice boards, which tell of its significance and history. I felt very sad when I visited it recently. The smoke scent from the fire had gone, along with the pride taken by the brother and sister in the simple room, with its dresser, which, in the old-fashioned traditional way, faced the fire so the plates and bowls sitting on the shelves gleamed in the light of the flames.

The president's ancestral cottage was the last one to be occupied in an ancient settlement type called a clachan. A clachan is a group of dwellings, which usually housed an extended family, who stayed together for defensive purposes and co-operated in working the land.

Clachans were usually adjacent to a good water supply. In the past, there was no proper sewage system and water came from a well, a nearby spring, stream or river. Folklore records that choosing a site for a dwelling within a clachan was simple: a hat was thrown up into the air on a windy day and the house was built wherever it landed. That was sensible because the hat invariably came down on a comparatively sheltered spot. Another consideration was that the new dwelling should not be in the line of fire, so to speak, of waste flowing from a cottage above.

Water was very precious. It had to be carried in buckets from its source and was stored inside the cottage in buckets, which were lined up in a row beside the external door. The farmer's wife used the water as economically as possible. She would have washed the dishes in it, followed by clothes, the fireplace and the floor. As she had no place to empty the bucket, she'd have poured the dirty water carefully out of the door, making sure she didn't annoy the fairies by throwing it round them.

Having a bath was a problem. Traditionally, Saturday night was bath night. A large tin bath was pulled up in front of the fire and filled with cold water, which was warmed by kettles full of boiling water that had been heated on the crook and crane hanging over the fire. The family took turns to get into the bath and wash. It would have been impossible to have any semblance of modesty in a one-roomed cottage, which might have housed seventeen family members. As each person climbed out of the bath a small burning ember from the fire was placed in the water to sterilise it. By the time a large family had bathed, the water must have looked like soup!

There are the remains of many clachans scattered around the Tyrone countryside. Many, like the old Woodrow Wilson homestead, are unoccupied. Others have one surviving branch of the family living in a single dwelling. In the past, there could have been fifteen, or more, families living on the site, but the others either died or emigrated. The Great Famine had a devastating effect on the population. The Wilson homestead, in common with other clachans, has the remains of other old dwellings on-site, some of which have been recycled as housing for animals.

The old Woodrow Wilson homestead is a sturdy stone dwelling, but not all dwellings in clachans were built from stone. Pre-famine pressure on the land, caused by the large population, was such that many cabins were built of sods of earth. They had a lifespan of approximately ten years. Another interesting type of dwelling, which has disappeared but was once common throughout the western fringe of Europe, was the byre house where the cows shared the living space with the owners. An example of a typical byre house, originally from County Donegal, is preserved at the Ulster Folk and Transport Museum at Cultra in County Down. It is a one-roomed dwelling built from local granite,

'Saturday night's bath night.'

with a thatched roof, a door in the middle of the wall and a single window to the left of the door and a deep trench to the right.

Sheep have warm, woolly coats and can survive outside during winter but cows need protection so they must be brought indoors. They were driven into the byre house and kept on the side of the room away from the fire. The trench caught their excrement, which was dug out and used to fertilise the land during spring. Manure was a precious commodity because crops could not grow well without it. Having it indoors was practical because it could not be stolen! The inmates of the house would have to get used to the smell. The sheltered animals also provided a source of heat.

29

ULYSSES S. GRANT AND COUNTY TYRONE

Thanks are due to the late Isabella Simpson, who I met in 1974 when she was living in the old Simpson homestead. She said she was 86 years of age. She told me about her connection with Ulysses Simpson Grant and her experiences during the time she worked as a nurse for the Mellon family, the wealthy banking family whose ancestral homestead forms part of the Ulster American Folk Park.

The maternal ancestors of Ulysses Simpson Grant (eighteenth American President, 1869–1887) lived in a small, two-roomed farmhouse with a mud floor at Dergnagh, off the old road between Dungannon and Ballygawley, County Tyrone.

I first visited the old homestead in the early 1970s, when I met a member of the Simpson family, Isabella Simpson, who lived there. She died in 1978, leaving her farm to Jackie Simpson, who was the last male member of the family to have been born there. He sold the property to Dungannon District Council. It came into public ownership in 1983 and was restored.

The Simpsons emigrated from Scotland to County Tyrone during the sixteenth century during what is known as 'the killing times' because Presbyterians were being persecuted because of their faith.

During the nineteen century, the cottage associated with President Ulysses Simpson Grant looked as if it had been built during the eighteenth century because it seemed to be built of stone. Local folklore said Simpson family members were among the first settlers in Tyrone, who arrived during the sixteenth century. Houses belonging to the original sixteenth-century planters had mud walls, reinforced with reeds. The restorers were delighted to find large sections of mud walls and an original mud-and-wattle canopy fireplace which dated the old home to the fifteenth century! So the folklore was correct! That's one of the amazing things about folklore – it often turns out to be correct, although it flies in the face of apparent facts.

President Grant's ancestors left Ireland during the mid-eighteenth century, so the old farm and home have been restored to look as they would have done at that time. The house has two rooms, mud floors and the type of furniture in vogue at the time. There is a settle bed and a dresser inside while outside there is a horse-drawn cart, along with turf creels and ploughs of the period.

Ulysses Simpson Grant's maternal grandfather, John Simpson, was born in 1738 at Dergnagh. He migrated to Pennsylvania when he was 22. His daughter, Hannah Simpson, married Jesse Root Grant and Ulysses Simpson Grant, the eldest of their six children, was born on 27 April 1822 in Point Pleasant, Clermont County, Ohio. He didn't like his given name, which was Hiram Ulysses Grant, so he changed it when he trained as a soldier in West Point to Ulysses S. Grant. The 'S' stands for his mother's maiden name, Simpson, although his fellow cadets called him 'Sam' for 'Uncle Sam' Grant.

Ulysses was Commanding General of the United States Army from 1864 until 1869. He was an excellent leader who gained international recognition during the American Civil War. He was regarded as a hero and was elected President in 1869.

I find him amusing because he, probably unconsciously, displays his Ulster-Scots (Scots-Irish) characteristics. For example, while campaigning for a second term in office in 1872, he was attacked by Liberal Republican reformers. His response was to say they were 'narrow-headed men with their eyes so close together they can look out of the same gimlet hole without winking'! Both sides of the community in Tyrone describe the other as 'having their eyes too close together'!

Ulysses spent five days in Ireland during 1879. He travelled by rail from Dublin to Ulster, with overnight stays in Derry/Londonderry and Belfast.

I find it surprising, as did Isabella Simpson, that he didn't visit his ancestral home! He appears to have been proud of his Irish ancestry, but perhaps he didn't want to draw attention to the poor conditions his grandfather had left? I remember the conversation I had with her very well. She had served as a nurse to the Mellon banking family, who she said were delightful employers and very proud of their ancestral home.

Judge Thompson Mellon was born in 1813, the son of Andrew and Rebecca Wauchob, Ulster-Scots farmers who lived at Camp Hill, Cappagh, County Tyrone, before migrating to Pittsburgh. The Mellons were very interested in their old family homestead. Thomas Mellon's grandson, Matthew, was instrumental in acquiring it and it now forms a nucleus for the foundation of the Ulster American Folk Park, along with the Mellon Centre for Migration Studies near Omagh, County Tyrone.

Ulysses Simpson Grant's visit to Ulster was in stark contrast to the quiet contribution to Tyrone's cultural heritage by Matthew Mellon. He was a showman. His visit to Ulster attracted large crowds that could be compared to a travelling circus. When he spoke to a crowd outside Belfast City Hall, he said, 'I am by birth a citizen of a country where there are more Irishmen, either native born or the descendants of Irishmen, than there are in all of Ireland.'

Ulysses Simpson Grant visited Belfast's Harland & Wolff shipyard during January 1879. It was the world's largest single shipyard at the

'Yer man's flyin' tonight!'

time. He was accompanied by Belfast's Mayor John Browne and welcomed by 2,000 workmen who gathered around his carriage shouting, 'Three cheers for Grant!'

In Coleraine, Ulysses spoke about the close ties between the Irish and Americans. He drew an 'immense crowd' in Ballymena and a cheering crowd of about 1,000 people came to see him in Portadown. In Derry/Londonderry, his party had difficulty getting through the throngs waiting to see him go to the town hall ceremony, where he received an honorary citizenship and where he signed the roll, making himself 'an Ulster Irishman'. At a banquet in his honour at Derry/Londonderry's county courthouse, Ulysses Simpson Grant said Irish entrepreneurs should invest in the United States to avoid the payment of controversial US tariffs on shirts and linen. They were the mainstays of Derry/Londonderry's economy. He said that there was plenty of room for Irish emigrants in America.

Ulysses Simpson Grant was an alcoholic who smoked twenty cigars a day. He died from throat cancer on 23 July 1885. His death caused early speculation about a link between cancer and smoking.

In Ulster, Presbyterian planters have the reputation of being straight-laced, stubborn and honest, even though they made their own alcohol and drank a lot – smoking and heavy drinking were acceptable in those days. Many old clay pipes have been found in the fields around the old homesteads. Ulysses Simpson Grant was following tradition by smoking and drinking a lot. It has been said that his struggle with alcoholism helped him understand and discipline others. It was one of the characteristics that made him a great leader and he was always sober when he needed to be. Unfortunately for him, he did let people who mattered see him drunk, which had a negative effect on his early career.

30

TYRONE AND IRISH COFFEE

I usually avoid Irish pubs outside Ireland because they are so pseudo, but I saw one on the waterfront in San Francisco that looked really nice, so I went inside.

It was a long way from Ireland to San Francisco. I was jet-lagged and in need of something to pick me up. I started chatting to the bartender and discovered he was also Irish. During our conversation about a good 'pick-me-up', I confessed three things have a tendency to upset my stomach – coffee, cream and whiskey – but Irish coffee's fine! He suggested that in that case the best thing a woman in my jet-lagged condition could do was have an Irish coffee. I agreed and listened intently as he told me that Irish coffee was born in San Francisco. I argued that if Irish coffee had been invented in San Francisco, it would have been called San Franciscan coffee. The bartender countered that it was made with Irish whiskey, hence the name. I didn't argue any more, but inwardly thought, 'That can't be right.' Several years later, thanks to information I found in Castlederg library, I was delighted to discover that Irish coffee is not an American invention! It was the brainchild of a Tyrone man called Joe Sheridan, who was born near Castlederg in Bridgetown in 1909 and had a burning ambition to become a chef. In 1943, he applied for, and got, the position of chef in a restaurant in Foynes. It was one of the top restaurants in Ireland and was situated in the terminal building of Foynes Airport, a small airport on the coast, near Limerick. Chef Joe catered for passengers on early transatlantic flights.

During the Second World War, flying was dangerous so Joe's clients were usually not only weary and jet-lagged but also frightened. The Republic of Ireland was a neutral country, but Germany didn't always respect that neutrality and attacked it on several occasions.

One night, late in the winter of 1943, a flight set out from Foynes to Borwood in Newfoundland. The weather was so awful that the captain decided the safest thing he could do was turn round, return to Foynes and hope to set out again when conditions improved.

Joe was contacted, along with other members of Foynes' airport staff, and asked to prepare something warm and comforting for the passengers. On the spur of a moment, he added a spoonful of brown sugar to the coffee, some whiskey and floated whipped cream on top. (Pouring whiskey into coffee, or tea, is an old custom often found in Ireland and in the Highlands of Scotland.) The passengers enjoyed their treat and afterwards one of them came to Joe, thanked him for the wonderful coffee and asked, 'Is that Brazilian coffee?' Jokingly Joe replied, 'No, it's Irish coffee.'

Joe started thinking about Irish coffee. The more he thought, the more he felt the presentation needed to be improved. Several weeks later, he made Irish coffee in a stemmed glass. He thought it looked good, but wanted a second opinion, so he took it to the owner of the Foynes restaurant, Brendan O'Reagan, and asked, 'How's that for presentation?'

'Sheer genius, chef! Sheer genius!' came the quick response.

It is said that:

The cream is as rich as an Irish brogue,
The coffee is as strong as a friendly hand,
The sugar is as sweet as the tongue of a rogue,
With whiskey as smooth as the wit of the land.

The airport in Foynes was closed in 1946 and replaced by the new Shannon International Airport on the other side of the River Shannon. Joe Sheridan became chef in the new airport's restaurant. He brought his famous drink with him and it is still served to VIP passengers.

In 1952, Joe Sheridan was offered a position at the Buena Vista restaurant in San Francisco, where he introduced his customers to Irish coffee. He is buried in Oakland, California, and a memorial plaque at his graveside is inscribed with the words, 'Here lies Joe Sheridan, the inventor of the world's most famous drink: Irish Coffee.' That is undoubtedly the reason the bartender I met in San Francisco was convinced the Irish coffee originated there. It didn't! It originated in the mind of a genius born in County Tyrone.

31

THE HOKEY COKEY

I always thought 'The Hokey Cokey' was one of those traditional jingles, such as 'Ma! Ma! Would Ye Buy Me a Banana?' and 'Wee Willie's Lost His Marble', which are loved by Irish children of all ages. I was amazed to find it was written by Jimmy Kennedy, one of the greatest songwriters of all time, who was born at Pretoria Terrace, Omagh, on 20 July 1902. He wrote the lyrics of more than 2,000 songs, including 200 that became international hits and 50 all-time classics, such as 'The Hokey Cokey' and the evocative 'Red Sails in the Sunset'.

I love the story behind 'Red Sails in the Sunset'.

Although he moved to London Jimmy never lost his love of his home and returned to visit his family at every available opportunity. One of his favourite occupations was sitting, with his young sister, watching the sun go down over the sea. She used to say that when the sun touched the sea on the horizon there would be a 'big sizzle'! One evening, as he sat watching, waiting for the 'big sizzle', the sailing ship, *Kitty of Coleraine*, sailed across the harbour. Jimmy found himself repeating the phrase 'red sails in the sunset' over and over again and was inspired to write one of his most famous songs:

Red sails in the sunset, way out on the sea;
Oh, carry my loved one home safely to me.
She sailed at the dawning, all day I've been blue;
Red sails in the sunset, I'm trusting in you.

Folklore provides a more prosaic inspiration behind another hit, 'Harbour Lights'. Apparently Jimmy got lost one night while driving his car. He stopped to try to find out where he was and his car head-lights illuminated a pub called Harbour Lights!

He wrote the lyrics of 'The Teddy Bear's Picnic', 'Hang Out Your Washing on the Siegfried Line', 'Down Mexico Way', 'My Prayer', 'The Isle of Capri', 'Love is Like a Violin' and 'Roll Along Covered Wagon'. Jimmy Kennedy had more hits in the United States than any other Irish or British songwriter until the duo of Lennon and McCartney – in other words, to put it into local parlance, he was 'some pup'!

Jimmy's father was a policeman, Constable Joseph Hamilton of the RIC. His mother, Anne Jane Baskin, originally came from Ardara in Donegal. In spite of having a father who had had such a practical, down-to-earth job, Jimmy's family was very creative. His maternal grandfather was the poet William Allingham from Ballyshannon and his grandmother Helen was a well-known Victorian watercolour painter.

Jimmy loved Tyrone's beautiful countryside. The chestnut trees in the garden around a family home in Coagh inspired him to write one of his first poems, 'Chestnut Trees'.

Jimmy's brother, Hamilton Kennedy, known as Hammie, was a BBC producer. He also became a famous songwriter. His hits included 'How Can You Buy Killarney?', 'Old Faithful' and 'Shawl of Galway Grey'.

Both brothers retained a love for County Tyrone, finding inspiration from the memory of its beautiful landscape and the character of its people throughout their lives.

32

JAMES BUCHANAN AND COUNTY TYRONE

George Buchanan came to Ulster and settled at Deroran, near Omagh, in County Tyrone, in 1674. One of his descendants, James Buchanan became President of the United States and is recorded as saying, 'My Ulster blood is a priceless heritage and I can never be too grateful for it.'

James Buchanan (fifteenth American President, 1857–1861) was born at Cove Gap, near Foltz, a small Ulster community in Franklin County, Pennsylvania. The family ancestral homestead in County Tyrone still exists but is not open to the public. It is marked by a blue plaque and now forms part of a larger dwelling.

It is said that the Buchanan family left Ulster because the future president's grandfather couldn't see anything but famine and a lack of religious freedom for Presbyterians in Ireland, so he set sail for 'the land of the free'. Crossing the Atlantic was hazardous in those days. If a cross had been erected on the Atlantic Ocean for every person who died while attempting to emigrate, the ocean waves would resemble a closely packed graveyard. Conditions on board ships were terrible. They were infested with rats. There were no proper toilets or washing facilities. Passengers were often short of food and water and they became diseased and died like flies. The Buchanans' small sailing ship was buffeted by a huge storm and forced to return to land for repairs after nine days at sea. When it was re-fitted, it set sail again, made good speed and arrived at its destination after seven weeks on the Atlantic.

James Buchanan studied law in Lancaster, Pennsylvania, was admitted to the bar in 1812 and established a successful law practice. He had a gift for oratory, which led him into politics. He never married and remains America's only bachelor president, although he was once engaged to Anne Coleman, the daughter of a wealthy Pennsylvanian family. For some unknown reason, he broke off the engagement. Anne Coleman died shortly afterwards. Rumour suggested she had committed suicide. Broken engagements destroyed reputations and a woman's reputation was very important. She would have been considered damaged goods and no longer suitable as an eligible marriage prospect and that could have been a reason for committing suicide, apart from the heartbreak.

When James Buchanan became president he made his twenty-seven-year-old niece, Harriet Lane, his hostess. She was a popular figure, who was called the 'Democratic Queen' in Washington.

It was unfortunate that James Buchanan became President immediately before the American Civil War. He did his best to negotiate a compromise between those who wanted to retain slavery and those who wanted to abolish it. He failed to realise that it's not the kind of topic on which it is possible to compromise. As a result, he ended up hated by both sides and is considered one of America's least successful presidents.

James Buchanan is said to have been America's first homosexual president. He lived in Washington DC for several years with Senator William Rufus King, a Democrat from Alabama, and the two men were inseparable. Their relationship was by no means secret and William King was referred to by many nicknames, including Mrs James Buchanan. When William was appointed minister to France in 1844, he wrote to James Buchanan saying, 'I am selfish enough to hope you will not be able to procure an associate who will cause you to feel no regret at our separation.' In a letter to a friend, James Buchanan said how much he missed William King's company, writing, 'I am now solitary and alone, having no companion in the house with me. I have gone a wooing to several gentlemen, but have not succeeded with any one of them.'

James Buchanan's family burnt his correspondence after his death. I wonder why? Did they prove that he was what would, in Tyrone of old, have been referred to as 'a bit of a ginny'?

33

DAVY CROCKETT AND CASTLEDERG

Thanks are due to the library staff in Castlederg, Roy Arbuckle, Joan Howlett and the late Tom McDevitte for information, the bartender in Lavery's pub, Castlederg, and the three delightful elderly gentlemen who shared a bit of craic *with me and the other 'innocent bystanders' I met in Castlederg.*

My friend Joan Howlett, who was born near Castlederg, says that when she was growing up it was a well-known, local fact that Davy Crockett's ancestors were from the vicinity. My old friend, the late Tom McDevitte (Barney McCoo), once told me the same thing, so my husband and I went to Castlederg to chat with some of the locals and hopefully find out something more about Davy Crockett's ancestors.

We arrived in Castlederg at lunchtime and, as always, put subsistence before research, so we stopped and asked a friendly local in the street if he knew somewhere nice to eat. He suggested the nearby Red Pepper restaurant. It looked lovely, so we took his advice.

There was an elderly gentleman sitting in a corner near the door. He was glancing around and looked friendly. I guessed he'd be willing to chat and started a conversation in the well-known Irish way by making derogatory comments on the weather. He agreed that it was abominable, 'proper desperate'. I asked him if he knew anything about Davy Crockett. He replied, 'You mean yon big man with the funny hat? Sure, I know nothing about him, but there's a fella up the street, owns the pub about a hundred yards up yonder, who knows all there is to know. Go in there and ask him. If he can't tell you, he'll give you contacts.'

I followed his advice and found the pub. The owner laughed and said he knew nothing but he very kindly wrote contacts down for me.

Three elderly gentlemen were sitting together, confabbing and drinking pints of beer at the bar. One of them smiled and said, 'The only thing I know about Davy Crockett is that he was behind the walls at the siege of Derry.'

Another said, 'Ye auld fool, ye! Yon wasnae Davy Crockett. He was killed at the Alamo in a battle with them Injuns. He was a young man when he died. He wasnae over a hundred years of age! Yon one in the Siege of Derry was his grandfather. A lot of people emigrated after that.'

'Well,' replied the first man, 'I know nothing about the Crocketts, but I can tell you a story. Would you like to hear it?'

I always love hearing a story, so said I would. I have no idea of where this story originated, how old it is or anything about it. All I can say is it's a good story and I heard it in a pub in Castlederg, County Tyrone.

'There was a man who had a wife who had a pet cat. He hated the cat, so one day, when his wife wasn't looking, he decided to get rid of it. He put it in his car, drove 20 miles away, chucked it out the car's window and drove home. When he arrived, there was the cat, looking very contented and smug, licking itself beside the fire. The man was astonished, but didn't say anything.

'Next day he decided he get rid of that annoying cat, so he grabbed it, shoved it in his car, drove 40 miles and threw it out the window. When he arrived home, the cat was as before, sitting looking smug in front of the fire and licking itself.

'The man decided he must make a big effort and get rid of that cat, so the next day he took it 80 miles away and threw it out of the car's window. Unfortunately, he had difficulty in finding his way back home, eventually realising he was completely lost and driving around in circles. He phoned his wife and asked, "Is the cat home yet?" She said, "Yes, it's looking very pleased with itself, sitting by the fire, purring contentedly and licking itself."

'"Well," he said, "will ye put the vokin' cat on the vokin' phone 'cos I'm vokin' lost?"'

'David Crockett? Ye mean yon big man
with the funny hat?'

Of course that has nothing to do with Davy Crockett, but it is the
type of story heard when locals are sitting around, having a bit of *craic*.

The red men roamed freely in the American wilderness long before
white men. Kentucky and Tennessee were a kind of no man's land.
There were a few traders, commonly known as 'the long hunters'
because they spent long periods of time in the backwoods, trapping
wild animals, such as beavers. The stories they brought back inspired
many families of Ulster descent up the Shenandoah Valley and down
into Tennessee.

John Crockett emigrated to America with his parents, grew up in
Tennessee, married and started a family. His son Davy was born in
a pioneer mud cabin in 1782. They were very poor, so John Crockett
hired his son out as a labourer to his neighbours, resulting in Davy

Crockett having little education. He became involved in the war against the Creek Indians, gained an excellent reputation as an Indian fighter and was awarded the title 'King of the Wild Frontier'. He was a popular, natural leader which led to his election to the Tennessee state legislature. He served several terms but was finally defeated in 1835, after which he headed to Tennessee and joined the American army fighting the Mexicans. He died at the Alamo on 6 March 1836 when the United States army was overwhelmed by large numbers of Santa Anna's army and I must confess that I still don't know much about his connection with Castlederg!

GLOSSARY

AHAGUR	term of endearment (from Irish '*a théagar*')
AMANG	among
ANGLEBERRIES	a type of growth, caused by a virus, that grows on horses and cattle
ARRA	an exclamation
AULD	old, as in 'she's an auld doll' (old woman)
AVICK	son, as in 'right you are, son' (from Irish '*a mhic*')
BAITH	both
BATE	get the better of, as in 'I'll bate ye!'
BATES BANAGHER	Banagher did an unbelievably fantastic thing: he bate the devil, hence the saying, 'that bates Banagher and Banagher bate the devil!' (possibly in Banagher Glen, Roe Valley, County L'Derry)
BEGOB	exclamation; today young people would say a naughty word that rhymes with duck!
BEGORRAH	exclamation; see above
BEEK	warm oneself
BIGGIT	built
BLACK MOUTH	Presbyterian; many Presbyterians were very poor so they ate blackberries, which dyed their mouths black
BLATTERED	hit, as in 'She blattered him with a rolling pin!'
BLOUTER	hit
BLUR-AN-AGERS	swear word; blood and thunder

BONNIE	pretty
BOYO(S)	literally, boys, as in 'Them boyos are quare an' crafty!' (Those boys – they could be old men – are dishonest)
BREECHES	trousers
BIRRIED	buried
BLUTTERED	drunk
BOWLTS	bolts
BURNBRAE	slope with a burn (stream) at the bottom of it
BUSTED	broken
CAULD	cold
CHILDER	children, as in 'Min' the childer for me' (Look after the children for me)
CHUCKED	tickled
CLABBER	mud, dirt, as in 'Them boots is covered in clabber' (from Irish 'clabar')
CLANER	cleaner, well brought up
CLATTY	dirty, untidy, as in 'She is quare an' clatty'
CLOUT	cloth, item of clothing, as in 'Hand me a clout til ...'
COITE	small boat
COTHAMORE	a type of overcoat (from Irish 'cóta mór')
CRAITUR/CRATUR	this has two meanings, depending on context, 'Wud ye like a wee drop of the craitur?' (Would you like a drink?) or 'The poor wee craitur' (The poor child or animal)
CREEPY STOOL	a small, three-legged wooden stool, often used by babies who were learning to walk (to creep) by being pushed around the floor; having three legs enabled the stool to sit steadily on an uneven floor
CUT THE BUCKLE	dance
DEAD ON	excellent, 100 per cent, as in 'Yon wee lad's dead on!' (That boy has an excellent character)
DEIL	devil, as in 'I'll knock the deil outta ye' (I'll stop you being annoying)

DILSY	foolish woman, affected overdressed woman, social climber
DISAYSE	disease
DRUID	a Celtic priest
DURE	door
EEJIT	fool, 'Ye're a right eejit, so ye are'; 'eejit' can be used in an affectionate or a derogatory fashion, depending on the context and the tone of voice
ELF-SHOT	cursed, 'Yon wean's elf-shot!' (That child's not thriving)
FASH	fuss, get upset, 'Don't fash yersel'!' (There's no need to be upset)
FLAFF	not being able to achieve anything, 'He was flaffing around'
FLIPERTI JIPPERTIES	worthless trinkets, 'Them's just a pack av flippers jipperties' (They are worthless objects); a fliperti-jippertie is an empty-headed woman
FORNENST	next to
FORRIT	forward
GAPE	stare, as in 'Yon auld deil gaped at me!'
GOB	mouth (from Irish 'gob')
GOXTY	exclamation; also, 'By gox!'
GRAIP	agricultural fork, as in 'Ah cannae find the graip!' (The agricultural fork is lost)
GRIG	merry, very lively person who is full of frolic and jest
GULDERED	shouted, as in 'She guldered at the weans' (She shouted at the children)
HALF-TORE	drunk, as in 'She was half tore'
HOT GOOSE	the type of iron that was heated in the fire, as in 'She got a bad burn from her hot goose'
HOOTER	mouth
INDIAN BAG	a bag used to carry coal; in the past, these bags were used by poverty-stricken people to wrap around their shoulders to keep them warm

INEXPRESSIBLES	trousers
KEEP YER PECKER UP	don't get discouraged, don't give up
KIFFLED	potter about, be indecisive, to 'flaff about'.
KIPPEEN	little stick, twig (from Irish '*cipín*')
KIRK	church
KNACKERED	exhausted
KNOCK THE MELT	fight, as in 'They knocked the melt outta each other' (They had a big fight)
LAZY BEDS	a labour-saving method of growing potatoes
LEANHAUN SHEE	a dangerous type of fairy (from Irish '*leannán sí*')
LEP	jump, leap
MAUN	must
MAWED	very old word meaning the sound a cow makes (moo)
MOOCHING	rambling around without a clear aim, as in 'He was mooching rou' the corner' (He was walking aimlessly around the corner)
MUMMERS	(also known as 'straw men') actors in a loud type of ancient folk play who are dressed in head gear that resembles basket-ware woven from willow
MUSHA	well! (from Irish '*muise*')
NOT IN A CONDITION TO BE FRIGHTENED	In the early stages of pregnancy
OVERLOOKED	cursed; see 'elf-shot'
OUL	old, 'She's nothin' but an oul' doll' (She's an old woman)
OXTER	armpit, as in 'It hurt my oxter' or 'She was right up the oxters' (She had made an effort with her appearance)
PASTIE	a type of 'delicacy' sold along with chips
PECKER	mouth, as in 'She has a pecker like a crow'
PISHROGUES	spell associated with evil
POITEEN	(also spelt poteen) home-made whisky (from Irish '*poitín*')

PURTIEST	best-looking, as in 'Yon sow's the purtiest A've ever seen' (That sow is the best I've ever seen)
PROPER DESPERATE	terrible, as in 'It's quare an' desperate!' (That's terrible)
QUARE	This can mean either 'very' or 'odd', as in 'He's the quare guid fella' (He's a very good man) or 'He's quare!' (He's odd)
RAISON	reason
RAMSCALLION	rascal, 'He's a right ramscallion' (He's a rascal)
REEK	smell
RIGHTLY BLUTTERED	very drunk
ROE	red
SCALPEEN	a temporary home for someone who has been evicted (from Irish '*scailpín*')
SETTLE ITS HASH	stop
SHEILING	a temporary home in a summer pasture
SHILLELAGH	stout cudgel cut from hawthorn, or oak, with a knotted end
SNICK	unbelievably clever person, 'She's nothin' but a snick!' (She's very clever)
SOWANS	type of drink made out of oats, used before tea was introduced
SOWL	soul, used as an exclamation, as in 'Indeed an' sowl!'
SPROCKLE	move with difficulty, 'She sprockled outta the chair'
STARVING WITH COLD	extremely cold, freezing, 'It wud have froze a fairy an' I was starving with cauld' (It was extremely cold and I was freezing)
STRUCKEN	struck
SWITHERED	dithered between possibilities
TARE-AN-OUNCE	exclamation
TEEMIN'	very heavy rain
THE GOOD PEOPLE	the fairies
THEEKIT	thatched
THEGITHER	together

THOCHT	thought
THONDER	over there
THRESHES	thrushes
TROTH	truth
TURNED	in the past people asked tailors to unpick garments, reverse the material and sew it up again, so it appeared like new
TWA	two
TWO ARMS THE SAME LENGTH	standing looking awkward or useless, as in 'The big eejit stood in the dure with his two arms the same length' (The fool stood in the doorway, looking awkward)
WEANS	literally, 'wee ones', children
WHAT THE DICKENS?	exclamation; today young people would probably say a naughty word that rhymes with 'duck'!
WHIRRO	exclamation
WHORL	whirl, 'Ma heid was in a whorl' (My head was in a whirl)
WUD	would
YER	your
YER MAN	Ulsterism meaning 'any man', 'See yer man' (Regarding that man), 'Look at yer man' (Look at him)
YON YONDER	over there, as in 'Luk at thon yonder!' (Look at that over there!)